Breakthrough Network Marketing Strategies For The Internet Age

Breakthrough Network Marketing Strategies For The Internet Age

David Vass

Co-authored by Doug Vass

Brought to you by: Zfreedom[TM]

iUniverse, Inc.

New York Lincoln Shanghai

Breakthrough Network Marketing Strategies For The Internet Age

iUniverse books may be ordered through booksellers or by contacting:

iUniverse
2021 Pine Lake Road, Suite 100
Lincoln, NE 68512
www.iuniverse.com
1-800-Authors (1-800-288-4677)

Because of the dynamic nature of the Internet, any Web addresses or links contained in this book may have changed since publication and may no longer be valid.

The views expressed in this work are solely those of the author and do not necessarily reflect the views of the publisher, and the publisher hereby disclaims any responsibility for them.

ISBN: 978-0-595-49359-3 (pbk)
ISBN: 978-0-595-61069-3 (ebk)

Printed in the United States of America

Contents

Introduction

Let me first thank you for your bold initiative in purchasing this important book. I promise that I won't waste your time and this could be the very breakthrough that you've been looking for in your quest to build a viable home business for yourself and your family.

You may have often heard the adage that, "you usually get what you pay for", but it's "usually" and not "always". In this case you are getting top value for the price of two cups of coffee.

I'm just so tired of the dead-end promises you keep seeing on the internet and the hoard of misinformation about multi-level marketing that you've probably heard about. Some marketers are even afraid of using the word "MLM" because of people's reactions. Even if YOU have had some bad experiences in this industry, I'm about to share with you a business model that has already won a lot of "nay-sayers" back.

You see, there is the *old* way of doing network marketing and there is a *new*, easier and more predictable way of practically guaranteeing success. This success was the domain of a few smart and savvy business owners but we've invested a lot of time and effort into this book so that you can know exactly how to succeed in MLM. Some people don't want these "secrets" out in the open, but we feel that you deserve to know the strategies top MLM'ers use to build their organization so that you can go and do the same!

This industry is plagued with big promises and few people who really reach their full potential. You also know that there are many who, without a college education, have become self-made millionaires.

Perhaps you are not aiming for the millions but you want the financial freedom that you deserve—the freedom to live life on your terms. My hope is that by the time you complete this book, you'll realize the power in your hands to literally change the course of your financial future.

An amazing discovery awaits you in these pages!

1

Squeezing Water Out Of Stones

If we were to take a look at the history of the network marketing industry, we can trace its start back to the 1940s when *Nutrilite Products, Inc.*, launched the sale of food supplement products. This would be followed about ten years later by *Amway* who introduced the sale of household products. For the next sixty years the industry has evolved into a legitimate channel for distribution of goods and services.

Together, network marketing companies generated **$28.7 billion** in U.S. sales in 2002, according to the Direct Selling Association (DSA), a lobbying association that represents network marketers and other companies who sell directly to consumers.

But the industry has not been without controversy. Plagued by illegal pyramid schemes and scam artists, poorly run companies, misguided distributors promising quick and easy riches to those who join … all enter to make a recipe for disaster.

In other words, many people have been duped in one manner or another by a MLM "opportunity" and never stick around long enough to find the "golden nuggets" among the dirt.

Simply because a company labels itself as a 'network marketing company' doesn't mean that your work of due diligence is done. Just think about it: If I approached you with a great stock pick would you just invest your money without checking out the company and product first? You'd be foolhardy to invest money without first knowing something about the company.

Here are some quick tips you can use to check out any new opportunity that comes your way:

1. **Make sure that a solid product or service is the foundation of the business.** This may sounds like a given, but in many pyramid schemes the product or service is only a cover-up for money passing from hand to hand. This money normally comes from exorbitant sign-up fees and the sale of a 'marketing kit'. Most people who get involved in these schemes will lose money because no new revenue comes in from customers, just distributors passing along signup fees.

The Ponzi scheme is another illegal "opportunity" which involves no products at all, but rather promises of investment or insurance windfalls. You can expect to pay anywhere from $20 to $90 as a signup fee for a legitimate business, but if there is no product or service being sold then hold on to your money and stay far away from such "opportunities".

2. **Pay only what you can afford to invest as a startup cost for joining the company.** Practically all network marketing companies will require you to make a minimum purchase to start as a distributor. If this seems too excessive to you, use this as a sign to stay away. This is not the time to go into credit card debt because you are swayed by the prospect of making back your money quickly. Any normal business takes investment, but you should not be required to buy things that you don't need for the business just to add to the company's profit margin (marketing tools and product are an example of a necessary expense).

3. **Ensure that the commission structure and the sales of products are related.** Since you are not an employee but an independent distributor, this means that your income comes from commission sales. You should then be making a fair percentage of the sales. If your commission checks are being eaten away by several different attached fees, then you know that you are being scammed. Study the commission structure and read the fine print carefully.

4. **Don't get carried away by high income claims.** Advertisers have an obligation to indicate that those who join a business opportunity can lose money and their testimonials may not represent the typical distributor. A legitimate opportunity doesn't have to hype the true income potential in order for people to see it's a great opportunity. And when income claims are made be sure you know what amount of that income represents actual profit.

5. **Find out if the network marketing company has any complaints lodged against it in the state's Better Business Bureau where it is registered to do business.** Normally, you wouldn't be the first to have problems with a company.

If you find legitimate complaints then you should be very wary of such a company. A company may even continue to do business as usual even when they know that there are legal proceedings against it which could send the company into bankruptcy. All it takes is for the existing company to redefine itself and start a new company under a different name. In the mean time, your money has gone down the drain.

6. **Ensure that the company has a clear guarantee. Any legitimate company will be happy to buy back any unused or unsold product from you as a part of their guarantee.** If a company refuses to guarantee your satisfaction with their product then stay away. What does this say about the confidence they have in their own products? You may be charged a "restocking fee" that runs around 10-15%, but unused inventory should be refunded upon your request.

7. **The length of time the company has been in business is another sign to watch for.** At least 90% of network marketing companies go under within the first three years. Now this is a double-edged sword because the first three years is the usual time period during which the company is at the "ground floor" level and you can benefit tremendously since less people know about it. For long-term stability older companies are a surer bet. Like picking a stock, you must be able to determine which companies are more likely to succeed and which might not. If you do decide to join a start up company then make sure it has good financial backing preferably with NO debt.

8. **Do your own due diligence.** You have to determine for yourself whether the company is a scam or not. Usually you can determine this by asking yourself some questions:

- Does the company sell a unique product that's fairly priced and not available in stores?

- Are these products or services consumable so there is the potential for re-orders? If you are looking at a one-time sale such as a water filtration system then you'll always have to find new customers to maintain your business.

- Can these products be easily copied by another company and create instant competition or are they patented or proprietary products?

- Does the company offer refunds to dissatisfied customers or distributors so you don't risk buying an ineffective product?

- Is the company armed with competent legal defense? In order to make sure that the company is doing business within the legal parameters set up by the FTC this is necessary and should be made available to you.

- Can you short-cut your way to the top by paying a lot of money? This is probably a pyramid scheme that you do not want to touch with a 10-foot pole.

If you can go through these questions and answer them to your satisfaction then you are well on your to making a great pick.

You can have the best seeds in the world but if plant them in the wrong type of soil you'd reap a poor harvest. The key point here is that if you use the best marketing skills in the world to promote the wrong opportunity then you'll get disappointing results. Get the right soil and the seeds will flourish.

I've found that 90% of your success in network marketing depends on the business you choose to promote. As long as you invest in a great company, you can have average marketing skills and still reap incredible results! Remember, you cannot squeeze water out of a stone!

2

Secrets To Your Success

This chapter almost never made it in this book because I wanted to remain as practical as possible and avoid the "self-help" type of talk about believing in yourself and training your mind for success and you know the rest.

I don't want to downplay the mental side of network marketing and there are a lot of books you can read that will help to build your inner spirit and drive for success. (You should read *The New Psycho-Cybernetics* by Maxwell Maltz, one of the best in the field.)

I've seen so many times where an individual's success was limited only by their low estimation of where they can really reach. According to James Allen, "You will always gravitate to that which you secretly most love. Men do not attain that which they want but that which they are." And Mike Todd once said, "I've never been poor, only broke. Being poor is a frame of mind. Being broke is a temporary condition."

What I'm trying to emphasize here is that YOU can be your biggest hurdle to your own success.

Mark Yarnell in his book, *Your First Year In Network Marketing,* writes, "Attrition is a considerable factor in our business. Yet we have rarely met anyone who has worked steadily in network marketing who doesn't eventually achieve success. And those rare individuals who do not succeed are usually their own worst enemies, constantly reinventing the wheel and complicating the simplest path to prosperity in the history of capitalism."

Yarnell goes on to explain that from his analysis an estimated 95 percent of those who survive in network marketing become wealthy beyond their wildest expectations. This shows how the mental side of network marketing seems to be fairly important after all.

Below I'll discuss some ways that you can be sure that you survive in this business.

Visualize Your Dreams.

Some people talk about writing down goals but I like to focus on your dreams. I'm sure that you may have heard this a hundred times but there is hard scientific evidence that visualizing your dreams and where you will be one year from now is very powerful. Psychologists refer to this phenomenon as the "power of intention". For example, Michael Jordan, the greatest basketball player of all time, used visualization to create a very powerful force that increased his own ability. Deepak Chopra M.D. and best selling author refers to visualization as seeing your dreams as a present reality even though they might not yet be actualized.

When we visualize our dreams it is one form of confirming our intention to carry it out and so there is an energy and power that brings them to past. Even if you doubt that this works still try to visualize your dreams every day … whether it be seeing yourself on a month long holiday or buying that lake house property you've always wanted or helping the homeless in your city … you will be amazed at the results!

It wasn't long ago that I visualized the kind of house I wanted. I wanted one that had an unobstructed view of the Rocky Mountains, backed onto a ravine, a walk out basement, a family friendly neighborhood, etc. Most of the people I knew at the time said, "dream on" (that kind of house in the city I lived had an extremely high price tag) and of course, I did just that. Within one and a half years I was living in the house I visualized!

Never stop dreaming. See your dreams as reality … believe that it can be done.

How Strong Is Your Motivation?

Dreams need to be supported like fruits on a tree. If your dream is to reach a consistent monthly income of $10,000, then you must have reasons why you chose that number. Maybe you want to send your kids to college, leave your present job, take a vacation or pay off high interest credit cards. The point is, the stronger your "why", the more likely you will succeed because you won't be discouraged from pursuing your dreams by little obstacles.

Many people join a network marketing opportunity just to get a family member "off of their case" so they can say they joined. What could you expect from such a distributor? There is no strong and compelling reason to start this business and failure is the natural result. Success happens usually when it is forced upon us and we have no other option—our ships are burnt and we must conquer because there is no way to return. We finally determined that we wanted another type of life and failure was not an option.

For some people their motivation is to spend more time with their family because they don't want to be a stranger to their children. Many are just fed-up of the 9-5 grind and want to skip the morning commute. Your "why" will go a long way in determining your success.

Remain Focused

As a kid I would use a magnifying glass to burn pieces of paper, wood and sometimes some unfortunate little insects. In order to get the sunrays concentrated enough to reach the ignition temperature, it required focus. I'd have to hold the magnifying glass at the correct angle to capture the sun rays and keep it a fixed distance from the object I'd wanted to burn. If I moved my hand around then it just wouldn't work.

It's the same for your business as well. You have to remain focused on your dreams and aspirations if you intend to get things 'heated up' to the point where you can start a marketing fire. Every business takes some time before you can be profitable and you should realize that the startup is statistically the toughest time. To use another analogy, a rocket uses up most of its fuel when it is launching, not while it is in outer space.

There are many network marketers (if you can call them that) who skip from one new opportunity to another and never seem to find one that 'works for them'. They never seem to come to the realization that it is not really the companies that don't work but rather themselves. It's hard to look at ourselves in the mirror and realize that we are the problem—not the product, the company, or the compensation plan—but us!

If you just hold on long enough you can actually fail yourself to success. According to scientist Neils Bohr, an expert is a man or woman who has made all the mistakes which can be made in a very narrow field. That should be an encouragement to you as you travel down this road.

Treat It Like A Business

If you wanted to start a franchise you'd be looking at investing $12,000-$3 million in startup expenses! This doesn't include other ongoing fees and royalties you'll have to pay to the franchise owner. There is no way that you'd open a McDonalds and allow it to waste away for lack of attention. Why? Because you know that you have a lot of money at stake.

Comparatively speaking, you'll never have to pay that much money to start a network marketing business and for this reason many people see this as a reason not to treat their opporunity like a real business. Their reasoning goes something like this: "So what if it doesn't work out, I'll only lose $200." But when you consider the amount of money that you can make as a network marketer compared to a franchise which may take five years before it's out of the red, then your attitude should get an immediate adjustment.

You should have a plan, be aggressive in your marketing and give your business the same attention as you would to anything else you would hope to succeed at.

Learn As Much As You Can About Your Business And Industry.

You would expect your doctor to keep up to date with the latest drugs and techniques in the field of his or her specialty. You shouldn't expect any less of yourself. Read the recommended magazines and books in the field of network marketing and attend workshops to rub shoulders with other network marketers. Research other websites and articles to see what other marketers are doing. Continue to hone your craft and become an expert in your field. This will create confidence in yourself and in your opportunity. Keep in mind that many professionals spend 7-10 years in college and still make less than $100,000 per year. If you take your business seriously this can be your monthly check!

You should know the company and the products that you are promoting like the back of your hand. This includes the compensation plan, history of company, its leadership and growth. This takes less time than taking one college course so don't begrudge the time it takes to internalize these few facts that will contribute to your success. You don't have to become an expert in every minor detail of the products but should know enough to speak intelligently about them. This could mean just knowing what the company literature has to say about these products.

Don't Try To Re-Invent The Wheel

There is a big temptation for people from traditional business to join a network marketing opportunity and think that they can just import what they know about marketing and apply this to network marketing. It would be fool hardy to ignore what other successful people have been doing in your company and just go at it on your own. This doesn't mean that you cannot try to be innovative but it's always easier to copy examples of success rather than re-invent it.

If you are new to network marketing you should first try to learn from your upline before you venture into new waters. If your direct upline is also new to the business then you can always continue going up until you find some level of leadership that will be able to train you in the business.

Sometimes even before you join an opportunity you may have to investigate and research if there is a group within a company that has good marketing techniques. The group that will provide you with support is where you want to be. This support will go a long way in determining your success. As you emulate the success of your leadership you can then adjust your marketing strategy to what works best for you.

3

The NEW Paradigm Shift

The network marketing industry is infused with many paradoxes. One of which is that it has produced many millionaires and at the same time over 60% of all new network marketers quit within their first year. Why are some people quitting when so many others without the advantage of a college education or even business training are pulling in six-figure incomes?

Traditionally, these millionaire earners were great communicators with charismatic personalities that could stand before hotel rooms filled with potential recruits and sell their Armani suits from right off their backs. The idea is that these "super sales people" made everything look easy but most people are afraid of even the word "sell".

In other words, you could also be a high income earner if you took the time to learn these same skills which included:

- Recruiting prospects on the phone
- Conducting home meetings
- Using fax broadcast and mailing post cards
- Using classified ads in newspapers and magazines
- Prospecting using toll free numbers with recorded messages
- Radio and TV ads
- Warm list marketing
- Buying generic leads from lead generation companies and marketing to them

The main problem here was that few people had the marketing savvy or the motivation to use these strategies and they didn't survive the first year in the business.

It turned out that "getting three, who got nine, who brought in twenty seven" wasn't as easy as that guy on the conference call or hotel meeting stage made it sound!

How could you build a million-dollar business without knowing anything about promoting or marketing your business? If you took a second look at the distributors who did really well in their marketing, you'll notice that they had some business experience BEFORE entering the network marketing field. When they joined the business they had the correct mindset and business "know-how" to achieve success. Most people who joined a network marketing opportunity had no training whatsoever in running a home business and it showed.

The few brave souls who stuck around and took the trial and error pathway to success usually became wealthier than they ever imagined. But they were the exception and not the rule. In other words, the high attrition rate of any network marketing business is the greatest challenge to overcome. Most recruits don't stay around long enough to achieve the level of success they envisioned.

It's of no wonder, if you just mentioned "network marketing" to the average person he or she will immediately start thinking about talking to strangers, bothering family members, passing out business cards and cold-calling leads on the phone only to be politely (and sometimes impolitely) dismissed.

The good news is that the internet has created a paradigm shift in the way network marketing is done. The internet which has affected every other area of our lives has changed this OLD way of doing network marketing in such a dramatic way that you don't have to be a marketing genius to make a sizable income. In fact, the whole purpose of this book is to introduce you to a business model and philosophy that could place your business virtually on autopilot towards success.

You are about to uncover secrets that less than 1% of the network marketing community know about. Imagine harnessing the marketing power of the internet to promote your business without having to bang your head against a wall—it's simply exciting! I've seen new network marketers who have created massive downlines in less than a year much to the amazement of the 'traditional' heavy hitters. What took 10 years to accomplish can now be done in 10 months, thanks to the internet, when used properly.

In other words, the internet has really leveled the playing field for the "small guy" to be successful because the same tools are available to all, not just those with the deep pockets.

Take YouTube™ as an example of this new trend. If you were interested in getting an audition as an entertainer, you may have to fly to Hollywood or New York City and hope someone will give you a hearing. Now you can just record yourself with a $100 video camera and post it on the internet for a real audience to vote on.

Even TV producers are taking clips from YouTube™ and other online video services and using them as a basis for TV shows! Who would have ever thought that a day like this would come? We are dealing with a consumer-driven market! And this is what network marketing has been all about from the beginning—the consumer.

Now you can get the attention of millions of potential customers on the internet where just a few years ago you'd have to spend thousands of dollars to get the same readership or exposure. However, just because there are hundreds of millions of people online doesn't automatically translate into instant success for you. Wouldn't it be nice if life was that easy?

The traditional approach to network marketing is caving to the NEW way. There is a paradigm shift occurring and those who take advantage of this shift can get filthy rich with a lot less effort. This is a bold promise to make but it is a very true possibility because of the leverage of the internet.

4

Principles Of Internet Marketing For Network Marketers

If you've ever seen a MLM company touting how you can join and be successful without doing any selling, then you know right away they are lying to you. How can a company that depends on the sale of products to consumers not sell? So why would they make such incredible claims? These MLM companies know that 99.9% of their target markets hate sales. We are intimidated by the whole sales process so the idea of not selling but still making money is very attractive.

Such companies typically don't last because everyone realizes sooner or later somebody has to sell and its usually the distributor—meaning YOU!

It turns out that when most people think of "selling" they think of the slick used car salesman who is trying to trick innocent buyers out of their hard earned money, or some fast-talker pushing his wares. Selling is often akin to begging—begging people to do you a favor and buy something from you.

Face-to-face selling can be intimidating and most people just don't do well this method of sales.

Obviously, the fear of selling is very real to most. A great part of this fear has to do with handling rejection. Nobody likes to hear "No!" because we interpret that rejection as a rejection of ourselves, not our products. And there is little comfort in knowing that you have to go through a 100 "no's" to hear a few "yes's". If you could find a way of filtering all those rejections and deal only with the "yes's" then a huge hurdle will suddenly disappear.

It is a well known fact that computers are better at handling rejections than humans are (at least, I've never heard of a computer getting its feelings hurt), and this saves a lot of non-productive time for people who utilizes them in their marketing. The marketing system on the computer does the sifting and sorting so that you only have to deal with people who are interested in what you have to offer.

Now instead of being the pursuer you can become the pursued. Instead of running behind your "warm market" to get them into your organization you can now have people seeking you. But how is all this possible? In this chapter we'll take a skeletal look at the answer.

The Internet Is The INFORMATION Super Highway.

There are some marketers who will argue that there is nothing "breakthrough" about the internet as far as marketing is concerned, it's just a new channel of communication. In a way they are right and in another way they are wrong.

Let's take a look at other media used by marketers. There is TV, radio, news print, magazines, etc., and they all demand a certain method of marketing that is dictated by how people hear your message. For example, with a radio ad it will have to be played several times over because you want the person listening to be able to remember or have time to write down the information.

With a TV ad you can just keep the 1-800-number on the screen for the full length of the commercial and you can also demonstrate your product in use. It's very clear that different mediums require different marketing approaches.

How do you class the internet? It's primarily a print medium but those who attempted to apply offline print principles to the internet found that the results were disappointing. It's also a video medium but attention span is much lower than for TV watching.

If you consider YouTube, you'll find that popular videos are seldom beyond 10-15 minutes long. When the "next channel" is just one click away and there is email, photos, newspapers, internet chat and a host of other services you cannot get with a television tube, the marketing game changes.

With the exception of the Super Bowl, people don't watch TV for the commercials. People also rarely listen to the radio to hear the latest ad. In the same way surfers come to the internet to find information, not with the intention to find your business. **The internet marketer must keep this foundational principle in mind and bait his marketing hook accordingly.**

Here is how you can capitalize on this principle:

- Write articles and post them on their website
- Maintain a blog
- Offer a FREE downloadable report or book
- Offer subscription to a newsletter
- Post informational videos on video distribution sites like YouTube™.
- Create an online forum

If you *give* before you *get* you can quickly build trust and *attract* prospects to you rather than *pursue* them. Once you build trust and confidence in what you have to offer then the next step becomes a million times easier.

For example, a real estate agent can provide free tips on how to secure a mortgage with the best rates, or how to prepare your home so you'll get top dollars for it. These "reports" build confidence in the agent's knowledge and expertise and prospects will likely choose this agent for their real estate needs. Of course this agent may be just as efficient as another competitor but he immediately stands out because he offers something of value upfront rather than first asking for value.

If you approach a prospect right away with your offer, you'll be just one voice in a crowd all shouting for attention. But when you choose to give value upfront then you immediately separate yourself from that crowd and place yourself in the prospect indebtedness.

You may need to read that last paragraph again because there is a ton of marketing wisdom wrapped up in it. If you think of yourself as just making money and not giving value to people's lives then any business you're in won't last very long. Call it a "karma" thing or what you will, but businesses that GIVE VALUE survive for the long haul over those who are just trying to make a quick buck.

Collecting Lead Information

We've already discussed about the importance of providing valuable information to your prospect before you try to sell them on your opportunity. But it's just as important that you try to follow up on these interests. Not every point of contact will allow you to collect your prospect's information.

For example, if you post articles to an article database you wouldn't be able to ask the prospect for their information. However, your article will have a link to your website where you can collect their email address and phone number. This link is normally placed in the article byline where you are free to give a plug for your business and qualifications.

All of your hooks must be "baited" and all your bait must have a hook inside it. **The importance of actively following up on your prospect is one of the most overlooked aspects of online marketing.** You cannot follow-up if you don't ask for their email address or phone number.

Many marketing tests have shown that prospects will need at least 7-9 marketing messages before they make a decision. If you are leading prospects to a website and not collecting their information then you are likely to lose that visitor forever. It should take several "No's" before you decide that you have lost that prospect.

Follow Up, Follow Up, And More Follow Up!

Many types of sales require multiple steps. There are few things that we buy on the fly and the more expensive the more time we need "to think about it". That's why it is so important to realize that your prospect may not have enough information at the start to make an intelligent decision whether to join your organization or not. The more information you can provide the more informed and less forced they feel about joining.

In fact, the more information we have about an item we are interested in buying the less "sold" we feel and the more in control of the situation we feel we are. In essence, we just sold ourselves! Go into any electronic store, for example, and observe the sales person who just answers questions and give as much information about an item and you'll see the salesperson who is at the top of his or her game.

People love to buy—or join your organization—but it may take several encounters with them before they decide to do so.

Keep in mind that at the time you contact an individual their minds may be preoccupied with other things. So your prospect cannot give your proposal the full attention that you may require. Therefore, the more often they are exposed to your offer the more likely they'll sign up.

Following up on a prospect means sending timely messages using an autoresponder service (and we'll talk more about this later) or getting them to your blog or to subscribe to your newsletter.

I know one very successful network marketer who sends out messages to his prospects sometimes 2 and 3 times per day! This might seem overwhelming but we are living in the age of attention and success goes to those businesses who win your attention. You have to keep your "name" before that prospect otherwise you'll fade into oblivion. It's just the nature of the beast.

Ask For Increasing Commitment

If a total stranger walked up to you and requested from you $10,000 you'd think that he was crazy or had mistaken you for Bill Gates. Almost all big commitment started with a smaller commitment.

Even YOU started with a small commitment! Ask your parents how they met and how you came about and you'll see that your 'life' started with maybe a glance in the right direction, then the exchange of phone numbers, a few dates, perhaps an engagement and wedding and there was the house and mortgage and you popped out not long after!

All human relationships take that same general path. Your best friend became your best friend through small commitments that led to larger ones. It's the same with marketing. You build trust by offering value at first, then asking for a small commitment, and finally asking for the larger commitment.

Now this doesn't mean that there is anything wrong with "going for the kill" for that big sale, but just keep in mind that your results will be far less effective than going for the smaller sale first. After you've had this first sale your next step is to ask for the upgrade.

This is the same method that is used successfully in TV infomercials. You are asked to call first (small commitment), then offered the $19.95 price, then finally they try to upsell you on the "extras" you can get ONLY this one time. Some psychologist refers to this as the "foot in the door technique" because of the stages involved in the entire process.

Many successful online businesses use this same technique by offering a one-month free trial or $1 limited period trial. In this way the value is offered to the customer with a discounted trial price. Some businesses may think that this will lead the customer to take advantage of them but this is a tried and true method that seldom fails.

In this chapter you've been given a lot of marketing wisdom within a small space so we must spend some time to 'flesh these out' so that you don't miss them. In the next few chapters that's exactly what we'll do.

5

Information Marketing

In the previous chapter we took a brief overview of the principles of online marketing. We discussed how it was important to provide information to your prospects because people come to the internet to look for information, not to be advertised to. In this chapter we'll take a closer look at <u>how</u> you can provide this information.

<u>Writing Articles</u>

Article writing for marketing purposes is not new because this strategy has been used by many professionals for decades now. A dentist, for example, may write for his local news paper on how to keep your teeth sparkling white and your gums perfectly pink in the hopes that when you need to choose a dentist you'll remember his name. He in effect becomes the expert and uses the newspaper to display his knowledge.

Writing for your local newspaper may seem intimidating and you may not be able to convince the editor that you have something of value to offer. Here is where the internet shines as the great playing field leveler: You don't have to convince any authority that you have something of importance to share because you can publish your thoughts and articles on your own website. Not only on your own website, but there are several article directories which are set up so anyone with a keyboard and an internet connection can make contributions. This is not to say that there is no standard of quality to meet, but the hurdles are just easier to jump over.

Now, even if you consider yourself a poor writer you can hire other writers to do this for you and simply attach your name to the article. Before you think of this as being deceptive, it's what referred to in the publishing industry as "ghostwriting". The majority of the best-sellers you see on your favorite bookstore shelves

19

claimed to be written by celebrities and politicians, were written by professional writers—ghostwriters.

If you decide to write an article for yourself, what are the quickest ways of getting this done? Here are some quick tips you can use to churn out an article with little effort:

1. **Share some tips**. About the easiest article you can write is one which simply shares some tips about a subject in your field. For example, an article title could be "10 Tips For Growing Bigger Tomatoes" or "Seven Ways To Get A Brighter Smile".

What makes these articles easier to write is that you don't need a thought connection between each paragraph. Each tip could be a paragraph and there is no need to maintain a "flow" as you would in other types of writing. In other words it's a *list* rather than an *essay*. Publishers know readers love such articles because they are condensed and easier to digest.

2. **Share what your article is about in the first paragraph**. You can use your subject line to attract readers but you want to use the first paragraph to tell the reader what the article is really about. This is the method used by journalist where they share with you the 5W's: who, what, why, when and where of the news item. This is a great place to tell the reader the problems your article will solve or how they will benefit as a result of reading the article.

3. **Create an outline for your article first**. Like any type of writing you should have an outline before you start fleshing things out. This will help you to organize your thoughts and also ensure that your article will read in a logical fashion. This outline will be the skeleton of your article on which you will hang the "muscles" and "tissues".

4. **Share illustrations and examples to prove your point**. These are really the "muscles" and "tissues" mentioned above. Just think about your favorite movie. I'm sure that you can give the plot or main story line of the movie in under five minutes, but if the movie lasted for just five minutes you'd feel robbed. It's the same with your article, your reader should be able to get the main points after reading but these points need some dressing up.

5. **Give value**. You may think of your article as bait to get your readers to the real meat, which would be to buy your product or join your business, but you have to

give value to get value back. If you are afraid that giving away too much will leave you with nothing left you can put this feeling to rest. It's natural to feel this way but it's not what really happens in practice. If you give value in your articles, not only will you develop a reputation to offer value, but your readers will come to expect value from your business.

6. **Write in simple and clear language**. Unless you are targeting other experts in your field, you have to keep your lay-readers in mind. Write the way you'd talk to these people if you had them right before you. Not only will this make your writing more engaging, but your message will have a greater impact. If your language sounds legal and wooden, then your readers will think that you and your business are boring!

Now these tips won't turn you into a first-class article writer overnight but the main point is that you are not trying to win a Nobel Prize in literature but get people into your business. Remember, a best-selling book is not necessarily the best written book!

As you continue to write articles and submit them to article directories or Ezines, people will "vote" for these articles by choosing whether to read them or not. Keep in mind that just ONE well-written article can bring you thousands of dollars in business for many years to come.

In the final analysis writing articles can help you:

- Brand yourself as an expert in your field
- Get free advertising through your resource box
- Boost your website traffic by increasing your Google PageRank™ and website popularity
- Increase your sales and profits

Maintaining a Blog

This is the era of the blogosphere. Even politicians are using their blogs in order to promote their candidacy. A blog is a little more personal than your usual website or other marketing material and requires a level of consistency not demanded by other mediums. Here are some quick tips that will help bring your visitors back to your blog more often:

1. **Make your posts something you will want to read**. In other words, don't waste people's time but offer ideas, advice or tips that your readers will find valuable. If you write junk, then people would read once and never return.

2. **Inject some personality into your writing**. This is the place where you are chief editor and writer so have as much latitude as you want. Your blog is as close and personal to an email as you'll get, so allow your personality (real or assumed) to shine through. You can afford to be edgy, crazy, witty, snappy, but NEVER boring.

3. **Use a catchy headline**. Your headline will be the most prominent (indicated by font size) that your readers will see so try to pull them into the rest of the blog post by making this interesting. A whole book can be written on headline writing alone as we'll discuss later, but for now your headline should indicate a major benefit to the reader and build curiosity so they'll want to read further.

4. **Use keywords related to your topic or interest so that the search engines will find you**. Keep in mind that you are not writing just for writing sake but you want to attract the right crowd to your blog. So if you are promoting vitamin supplements you have to use those keywords that people are using when they are querying the search engines. You don't want to over do it, but you must have those words seeded over your blog so the search engines can easily determine what your blog is about. Use these keywords both in your category names, headlines and articles themselves.

5. **Link to other blogs within your market**. If you link to another blog then that blog owner will likely link back to your blog. In this way you can become a part of a network that will generate both traffic and link popularity for your blog. The key here is that your readers may not even know about these other blogs and by linking to them you show that you are not afraid to be compared to other marketers your field. Intuitively you'll think that you are driving traffic away from your site but the opposite is true in practice.

6. **Better to write short blog entries more often than long articles less often**. You want people to have a reason to come to your blog often. The less often you post then the less often they'll return. Unless they a have RSS feed to your blog or are on your email announcement list so they know when you've made a new post, readers can forget that you exist. So chop up those great ideas you have into smaller bite-size pieces and post more often.

Offer A FREE Downloadable Report Or Book

What you are reading now is this strategy in motion. Offering your visitors an information-packed FREE book is another way to build credibility for your business and offer value upfront. The point again (which we cannot over-emphasize) is that you are exhibiting your expertise at no cost or risk to the prospect so that they can check out your business before they join.

The question now becomes: "What do I offer in this book?"

You don't want to give all the kingdom's jewels away but you must give enough value to prove that you know what you are talking about. Now there are some situations where you CAN give all the information away because you are not in the business of selling the information but the SERVICE.

Case in point: Let's return to our dentist and we can see that he or she can give you all the secrets about keeping strong healthy teeth but you'll still need the service of a professional to do the deep cleaning that you cannot do at home. There are other cases where your prospect may want to know 'how to' do something without wanting to do it themselves. For example, it doesn't hurt to know how to repair your car's engine but you will most likely take your vehicle to a professional mechanic for major repairs.

Here again, having a book with your name on the cover establishes you as an expert and sets you head and shoulder above the average marketer. Let me mention again that you don't have to write this book yourself. You can hire a ghost-writer.

Now if you decide to write this book there are few 'short-cuts' you can use to get this out as soon as possible. If you keep looking at the number of pages you have to write to get a decent book you may not want to start. But here are a few resources you can use to get the material for your book:

- Articles that you have written before

- Interviews that you have conducted. You can have these transcribed and publish them into book form.

- Research you have done in the industry.

- Your own personal journey to get where you are now. (Autobiographical info.)

This is by no means an exhaustive list but it does get you thinking and less intimidated at the task before you. And once you have an outline worked out half the battle is already won.

Offer Subscription To A Newsletter

Many of the points that we have discussed already, especially as related to maintaining a blog would apply to your newsletter. You want to write interesting articles that give valuable information and that's charged with your personality, but there is also another angle here. You can run a newsletter without ever writing one article!

Just think about the popular magazines and newsletter that you read; how many of the articles are written by the owner or editor-in-chief? Once you have a large and responsive list, other writers will be breaking down your door to get you to publish their articles.

To build your credibility you will want to contribute to the newsletter occasionally but you are not under the same pressure to "produce" as you'll be in writing articles and maintaining a blog. Of course, you can accept guest articles on your blog but you'll want to write the majority of these articles so the blog remains "you".

Another powerful reason for running an online newsletter or Ezine is that you'll be reaching your prospects in their inboxes where you'll get more attention than on the web. If you can get permission to "invade" your prospect inboxes (which is becoming more difficult as time goes by) then you have won a very important piece of marketing real estate.

Just one note of warning: Running a newsletter takes time and dedication whether you write often or not, so you should only use this strategy if you are in for the long haul. If you can pull this off you have a very effective tool to promote your business.

Using Online Video Portals Like YouTube™

With the increase in the number of internet users logging on through broadband access and the great leap in online video technologies, online videos are becoming a marketing force to reckon with. It's estimated that almost 65% of U.S. internet users now have broadband access, and that number is expected to continue to grow to 80% by 2010.

As mentioned earlier, people don't go to YouTube™ to view commercials. This means that you'll have to be very creative in order to first get attention then subtly guide the viewers to your website. If you set out to do a blatant advertisement for your opportunity then you won't reach far.

An easy way to create a popular video is to look at those videos that are already getting a lot of attention. Ask yourself what it is about those videos that make people want to view them. Usually they are a little 'wacky' and offbeat but you'll find that the bottom line is that they provide ENTERTAINMENT. As one well-known marketer always says, "People lead very boring lives and they want to be entertained." It's no surprise then why the entertainment industry makes so much money!

And it's the entertainment value that will determine how your video performs online. You see, the real power of videos is that the attention span of web surfers is measured in seconds. Videos, because of their multimedia nature, engage the viewers at more sensual (emotional) levels than just plain text and pictures.

Your videos will be an indirect way to promote yourself and your business. Keep in mind that the same videos you post on the video directories you may want to use on your blog as well.

6

Small Effort, Big Results!

Except for a few rare cases, you'll seldom find any one online marketing strategy that gets you a flood of success. Normally it's the trickles from different streams that lead to the huge river flow. This means that you cannot depend on any one method to achieve success. Simply because one method gives fewer results doesn't mean you can afford to ignore it.

In this section we will want to look at some other methods of marketing your business online often overlooked by the network marketer or home business owner.

1. **Offer Testimonials.** Have you ever used a product that impressed you? Then you can offer a testimonial to the owner and be sure to include your name and website address. Not only will you increase your link-popularity because you now have your URL on another site, but you can get direct traffic from that link. This is a very good excuse to place your link on other websites where both you and the other webmaster benefit.

2. **Participate in message board forums**. Most message boards would not allow you to post blown-out ads. But you are allowed a signature file where you can place a small classified type ad and your website link. Many search engines also index message boards, so again you can increase your link popularity.

    You will be surprised to know the amount of good traffic you can get from message boards especially if your posts are helpful. Just one post that a lot of readers find valuable will keep your post popular which means that a lot of potential eyes can see your website link.

3. **Offer a unique service.** There are many webmasters who have built considerable traffic to their website by simply offering a unique and often free ser-

vice. This is the idea of post-card sites, free web hosting and free email services. Some sites may host form-processing script and even offer free auto-responders. This is the rare case of "if you build it they will come". The key here is to offer a service that other web users will find valuable and useful and gently guide them towards your main business.

4. **Use a reputable search engine optimization company.** Search engines provide a doorway to your website wider than any other. A search engine strategy should be part of your overall promotion efforts.

    Be warned, however, that there are many companies out there that are promising what they cannot deliver. Just look up their company's website under the "search engine optimization" and see where they rank. If they rank highly then it's obvious that they know what they are about. No use selling secrets to growing bigger tomatoes if those in your garden look feeble. Common sense should tell you that they cannot do any better for you. So choose wisely!

5. **Use Pay-Per-Click (PPC) Search Engines.** PPC search engines provide a way of getting immediate traffic to your site rather than waiting for your website to be indexed and inch its way up the ranks. Designing an effective PPC campaign is getting more and more challenging since direct competition can drive bidding prices outside of your advertising budget.

    If you are on a small budget then you can use a tool such as http:// www.goodkeywords.com to find lesser used and therefore lower-priced words. You can then bid on as many as are relevant to your site. This would be more productive then using the more competitive and higher-priced keywords.

6. **Use Solo Ezine Ads.** Solo Ezine ads remain one of the most low-cost but effective means of advertising on the Internet. A solo ad is sent out by itself to the entire Ezine database and therefore gets good exposure compared to a classified ad.

    You can simply do a search engine query for Ezines in your market segment that offers solo advertising. You can also check out a site such as http:// www.litsz.com for a number of widely read Ezines. With over 300,000 Ezines published online you should have little trouble finding advertisement space.

7. **Offer low-ticket items at auction sites.** It's no secret that auction sites such as ebay.com receive a ton of traffic. If you offer cheap products you can build your customer list very quickly. You can then offer back-end products to increase your return-on-investment.

    At least this is one case of "If the mountain cannot come to Mohammed then Mohammed will go to the mountain". Go to where the traffic is and the traffic will follow you!

8. **Provide a Press Release.** Sending out press releases is one method that can get your website flooded with visitors over a short period of time. You can pay a company such as pressreleasenetwork.com to do a press release for you. You can never tell which online and off-line news network will pick up your story and give you that shot in the arm that you are looking for.

    If you need help in the writing of your press releases you may check a service such as ereleases.com. A press release is really a 'hidden' advertisement for your business under the cover of a news-worthy story. It takes some skill to get your release accepted by news agencies but when it works its like marketing magic.

9. **Use Google Adwords and other PPC Search Engines.** Google Adwords are what feeds the ads that show up to the left as 'sponsored links' on Google's search results. This is a type of PPC search engine except that you pay only after your ad is clicked instead of making a deposit. You are able to set your budget—how much you are willing to spend per day—so you can keep your spending in check.

    The same tips as applied to normal PPC will apply here, except that your position or ranking depends on more than the amount of your bid for the keyword. Google has gradually added more and more features and also provide their own free training so that you know how to effectively use their tools. There are also other marketers who are experts in using Adwords and you can check out their products if you want to make this a major part of your online promotion.

10. **Perform a linking exchange campaign with another webmaster to get incoming links to your website.** The number of incoming links from pages with high ranking can boost your own page ranking in search engines like Google. Determine your present linking popularity by going to http://

www.linkpopularity.com and then contact other webmasters to ask for a link exchange.

You should try and use all these methods, but even if you don't attempt all you should be engaged in *most*. This doesn't mean that you'll have to do all the work for yourself. There are some aspects of your marketing you may want to out-source to another company who has the know-how, but you'll want to be sure that you are getting the results that you are looking for.

If you find any method is taking too much time and money without showing jus-tifiable returns then you'll have to cut your losses and invest your advertising dol-lars where you are making profit.

Again, you'll learn quickly that there are no magic bullets but fair effort that brings fair results. As you consistently promote your business you'll see the cumu-lative results as time goes by. Remember, that Rome wasn't built in a day.

7

What You Should Know About Your Prospects

If you are a tourist about to visit a new place you'll at least want to read about the country of your intended visit. What language the people speak, their culture, religions and places of interest are areas you would research. What may be perfectly accepted within your culture may be disrespectful in another. You cannot totally predict all that you'll experience and if you did this, it may squash the excitement and anticipation but you should know enough so not to embarrass yourself.

The same goes for marketing as well. You need to know enough about your prospect so that you can target your marketing message to reach them most effectively. There is an entire marketing industry that spends millions of dollars each year accumulating lists of customers in different demographics for advertisers to send their advertisement to. If you've ever bought a vehicle only to start getting advertisement from car insurance companies then you know what I'm talking about.

It's no use sending advertisement for baby products to senior citizens. You'll want to target young parents who will be in need of these products. Sending the right message to the wrong crowd is wasting advertising dollars and time.

One of the most targeted crowds you can market to is former customers of your type of product. If you are selling golf clubs then the most likely person to buy are those who have already bought clubs before. That is why any business' most important list is their customers who have already spend money with them.

As a network marketer your most responsive list should be those who have already been involved in an MLM company before. But we'll talk more about this later. First we'll look at the typical things you will want to know about your prospects to make your advertising effective.

Your Prospect Is More Important Than Your Product.

Network marketers are often taught that it's very important to know their product inside-out and be enthusiastic about sharing this information. While enthusiasm goes a long way in selling, it can also get in the way of selling.

The average network marketer will start telling their prospects all about their company and products and the magic that it performs without even asking what the prospect is looking for. Many people think of the great salesperson as the well-dressed car sales man who employs some seductive sales pitch to get people into the car of their dreams.

On the contrary great salespeople are great listeners. They listen to what the prospect is looking for and then they show how their product can fulfill that need. If you never listen then you'll never know where the itch is so you can scratch the right spot.

For example, if you assume that your prospect wants to become a millionaire and use that angle to get them into your company you may find a strange resistance to your pitch that may be interpreted as just hype. As great as money is, it's not the greatest motivator for everyone.

Some people want more time to spend with their family and others are looking for recognition and the list goes on. You have to be prepared to offer a different angle if needed and you should be aware of what makes your prospects tick.

Always place the needs of your prospect above yourself and your company.

Consider this approach: *"Hi Mr Smith, I've been a part of this great opportunity that has really changed my life. What is it that you are looking to get out of XYZ company?"*

Now this may seem weak to the person who believes in the hard sell. Although it's not the most refined marketing sales pitch, it places the prospects needs and opinions above yours. In other words, it places them in the place of CONTROL and if they choose to join your company they would have sold themselves.

Even if you offer the greatest products since sliced bread, your prospect is still more important than your product. You need to ask him questions and actively listen. If you treat him with respect you'll see the difference in your marketing results. This respect means that you won't B.S. him or trick him in any way—you'll be honest and forthright. In the words of David Ogilvy, "The consumer isn't stupid, the consumer is your mother"

Who Is An Ideal Prospect?

After you've been marketing for some time you'll see a pattern emerging in the demographics of your recruits. What's the typical age, income bracket, sex, occupation, marital status etc.? You may not ask for all this information upfront but you may notice that most of your recruits are middle-class, with young families and looking for a second source of income to help make ends meet.

How this information helps is that when you sit down to write your advertisement you will keep this "ideal prospect" in mind and write as though he or she was sitting right across from you. On the other end of the table is the reader who feels immediately as though you are speaking to him personally. This is what makes for powerful advertising.

It's very common to hear TV advertisements which immediately single out their target audience by asking a very pointed question such as, "Do you suffer from migraines?" And then what follows is a product that should help you overcome this problem. If you are not a migraine sufferer or don't have a close associate who is, then you may not even hear the commercial. As one popular comedian said, "When you are moving, every object looks like a box".

General Needs To Target

Network marketing is really "relationship marketing", according to Robert G. Allen, author of *Multiple Streams of Income*. There is no way of avoiding dealing with people because people are your business. This means that you must understand the basic psychological motivators that make people "tick" or that's involved in decision making. When you bring a prospect over the line to join your company you are a facilitator in decision making.

A basic tenet of selling is that people buy based on emotions and then justify their decision based on logic.

Think of the husband that goes to the hardware store and makes an expensive purchase of a tool kit just to decorate his garage. In other words, his wife knows that he has no skill in using this tool because he hardly repairs anything around the house. But he is infatuated by the power that this tool gives him. He is therefore swayed by the pride of ownership of this tool rather than the work he intend to do with it.

After making his purchase he suddenly realizes on the way home that he must give his wife an explanation. This is the time that the logic kicks in and he now must find a reasonable explanation for spending a fortune on garage decoration.

Just think about the last time you made a purchase of an item that you had to own. If you really think about it, you'll realize that you made that purchase wholly based on emotions and then found a good reason why you bought it. Except for survival situations, most of the decisions we make everyday are based on feelings and emotions instead of logic.

These emotions that motivate us can be placed in two classes:
1. The promise of gain <u>or</u>
2. The fear of loss.
The fear of loss is actually greater than the hope for gain.

I once read of an experiment that was done where an electric company wanted to help its customers to conserve energy. This company found that when they approached the home owners with the prospect that following some conservational tips would help them <u>save</u> money, this wasn't as effective as showing them how much money they <u>lose</u> by not following the tips. The bottom line is that we would prefer to avoid losing $100 rather than gain an extra $100!

Here is a list of the general or universal human motivators that your product needs to appeal to:

1. To be healthy
2. To be attractive
3. To be wealthy
4. To be popular/recognized
5. To have security
6. To achieve inner peace/sense of self-worth
7. To have more free time
8. To have fun/entertainment

Here is the million-dollar secret that few people even seem to know, <u>people don't</u> <u>really care about your product or company EXCEPT that it is just a tool to help</u> <u>them achieve these eight goals!</u>

People want to know from the get go what's really in it for them. Everyone is tuned in to the FM station **WIIFM—What's In It For Me!** So if you get caught up in talking about your products and company achievement, you can be easily tuned out if you don't tie these facts into how your products can meet the needs of your prospect.

This is the very reason why you cannot get hung up on the features of your company or products and forget to point out all the benefits. Most people find it very difficult to tell the difference between a feature and a benefit. Features are what your product or service is like (facts and data), and benefits are the value derived from using or owning your product or service.

For example, below is the list of features (in bold) for Bose® speakers and the *benefits* those *features* provide, as listed at their website (*bose.com*):

Direct/Reflecting® speaker technology
<u>Experience life like spaciousness from a natural balance of reflected and</u> <u>direct sound—similar to a live performance.</u>

Nine full-range helical voice coil drivers for each speaker
<u>Experience the full spectrum of rich, life like sound without any crossover</u> <u>network.</u>

Stereo Everywhere® speaker performance
The remarkable result of proprietary Bose® technologies that produce balanced stereo sound over a wide area. <u>Experience consistent coverage</u> that's unmatched by most conventional speakers that radiate sound into the room in a single direction.

Helically wound aluminum voice coils
This Bose technology allows you to <u>enjoy room-filling music</u> from speakers designed for higher durability, greater efficiency and superior power handling.

Acoustic Matrix™ enclosure
<u>Hear clear, well-defined low frequencies</u> over the entire low-frequency spectrum, as speaker chamber noise is dramatically reduced.

Free-standing active equalizer
<u>Enjoy smoother, more natural balance and clarity throughout the audio spectrum</u>.

The only problem with this list is that it comes under the "features" listing but there is a mixture of features and benefits which is a perfect illustration that even big company advertisers don't realize the difference. (I've underlined the real benefits!)

All the physical characteristics and technology behind a product are simply features. What they do for the customer is the real benefit.

The "So What?" Test

A simple test you can use to pull out all the benefits from the products that you sell is to ask the question, "So what?" You can go down the list of features and ask that question and think about the benefit to the customer, not to the company. Let's take as an example the ingredients of a nutritional drink—Zrii. (Quoted from Zrii.com)

- Phytonutrients, amino acids, trace minerals, anti-oxidants, polyphenols, tannins, bioflavonoids—substances well-documented for their ability to promote cellular rejuvenation and overall vitality. *("So what?")*

- Ellagic and gallic acid, and emblicanin—polyphenols that may help to reduce cellular oxidative stress, destroy free radicals, and support the detoxification of the body. *("So what?")*

- Rutin, quercetin superoxide dismutase—substances that can contribute to amalaki's anti-oxidant, anti-inflammatory, and youth-promoting qualities. *("So what?")*

- Ascorbagins—"mighty molecules" that are shown to create a protective bond around their own rich source of Vitamin C molecules, making them more bio-available than synthetic varieties. *("So what?")*

When you read through this list which contains many great features (ingredients or physical qualities) you must then show what consequences these all have for the customer.

Let me just mention that sometimes when we are very familiar with our products (like companies are) we can assume that the customer knows just as much. With the list above you may assume that your customer must know the importance of vitamin c in the diet, but it's still better to spell it out:

"Vitamin C, also called ascorbic acid, helps to maintain healthy collagen in the skin, repair damaged tissue, promote healthy teeth and bones, and boost the immune system."

And keeping in mind that people respond more to 'fear of loss' than 'promise of gain' then it may be more effective to state what will happen to an individual who lacks Vitamin C:

"People who do not consume enough Vitamin C often develop the following symptoms: swollen gums, wounds that don't heal, easy bruising, and bleeding gums."

Now which of those statements was more effective in getting your attention? If you said the second, then you can appreciate how important it is that when you are presenting an opportunity to a prospect you include what that person can LOSE if they don't make a positive decision—not just what they can gain by saying, "yes".

Features, Advantages and Benefits

According to Neil Rackham in his groundbreaking book, *SPIN Selling*, all benefits are not created equal, and he prefers to divide benefits into two categories: *benefits* and *advantages*.

First we already discussed that features are the facts, data, or information about your product or opportunity such as "Company has been growing by 5,000 new distributors each week", "We have the only natural food drink in the industry endorsed by a world-renowned doctor" and "Our phone lines are opened 24-hrs per day, 6 days per week."

These types of statements just give the facts and lack any real degree of persuasion. But they are unavoidable because they tell what your product is.

However, according to Rackham, an agreement on a definition of "benefit" was harder to come by. Different sale books will have different definitions such as:

A benefit shows how a feature can help a customer.

A benefit must have cost saving for the customer.

A benefit is any statement that meets a need.

A benefit has to appeal to the personal ego needs of the buyer, not to organizational or departmental needs.

A benefit is something you can offer that your competition can't.

A benefit gives a buying motive.

Rackham and his team carried out a series of sale experiments and finally came up with his own definitions for this purpose:

- *Type A Benefit*—This type shows how a product or service can be used or can help the customer.

- *Type B Benefit*—This type shows how a product or service meets an *explicit* need expressed by the customer.

The Type A Benefit is the commonly held definition and Type B is that introduced by the author. He found after hundreds of sales presentation that the Type B Benefit had a significant effect on the successful outcome of the sale. He then labeled this as "benefit" and referred to Type A Benefit as an "advantage".

So, in other words when a benefit had no relation to a need that the customer had expressed then it simply becomes an "advantage" for Rackham. When the product or service satisfies a need EXPRESSED by the prospect, then that's a real benefit. He found the more benefits your product or service has, the more sales you will make.

Let's put this finding another way; All the great things that your product and opportunity does mean nothing to the prospects unless they meet THEIR NEEDS! If you find out what your prospect's needs are, then you are just a few strides away from the sales finish line. So the final definition as per Rackham would look like this:

Features: Describe facts, data, and product characteristics.

Advantages: Show how products, services, or their features can be used or can help the customer.

Benefits: show how products or services meet explicit needs expressed by the customer.

From these definitions you'll notice that the only way you can determine a benefit for the prospect over an advantage is to be in direct contact with them. The need must be expressed or definitely known for it to be a benefit according the definition.

8

How To Aim Right And Get It Right

Perhaps you've heard the story of the "perfect" marksman. It goes something like this.

A man was traveling through the woods one day and found several arrows stuck in huge tree trunks. To his amazement each arrow had hit the bull's eye of a target circle painted on the trees. He thought to himself that this had to be the work of a master marksman with super human ability. He finally caught up with a young lad and discovered that he was less than superhuman. This young man first shot arrows into the tree trunks from a close range and after the arrows were securely embedded he then painted a target circle around them! This way he could never miss the target.

As humorous as this story may sound, it's the same way that many people go about their marketing. They shoot first and then they aim!

In the previous chapter we've looked at what you should know about your prospects. Now, we want to take it one step further to show how you can best find the prospects who will most likely respond to your offer. You want as much as possible to place your offer before those who are in need of your product and also willing and able to become successful Network Marketers.

Traditionally every new distributor was taught to make their family members and friends their first line of attack. This is indeed your "warm market" until you find out the cold shoulders your closest family members can give you. I'm sure that you can agree that family members can turn out to be the most critical about your dreams because somehow they "know you" and already know what you will amount to. Sound familiar?

Before we get sidetracked into a family-bashing session, please take note that those closest to you will often give you good advice because they want to protect you. They don't want you to get hurt and so most people of an entrepreneurial spirit will always get those who think that they are just dreaming, and need to wake up.

Also, as Robert Kiyosaki stated in his best-seller, *Rich Dad, Poor Dad*, we are generally taught that the way to have financial security is to go to school, get an education, secure a stable job, work forty years and hope to have something set aside for retirement. This is so engraved in our Western psyche that to think of another path places you in the "crazy dreamers" bracket.

The bottom line is that your warm market may not be the best place to start because you are more likely to "get rain on your parade" than fuel in your marketing tank. Of course there are exceptions to every rule and a family member may turn out to be your greatest ally, but simply because a prospect is related to you doesn't make them a great network marketer. The network marketing gene has not yet been isolated!

If network marketing success is not in the genes where can you find it? Below I want to share with you the traits which the most successful network marketers seem to have in common:

1. **They are big dreamers**. You will seldom find anyone in this industry that has made it big and DIDN'T dream big. Just like in the story that we started this chapter with, if you aim for nothing you'll normally strike it. I've never met a network marketer who hasn't started his journey with big dreams and ambitions.

2. **They Are Motivated**. Call it inner drive, ambition or whatever you may, you cannot make it in this business unless you <u>have to</u> make it. Most people are impelled by business failure in the past, personal setbacks, huge debt and a host of other "motivators" but there is something about the human spirit that causes you to find success when you have to. People who hit the millions normally have some story in their past that indicated that they may have failed several times before they hit the "jackpot".

3. **They implement new ideas quickly**. Successful people act fast and change their minds slowly. They are decisive and remain accountable for the decisions they make. This doesn't mean that there are no mis-

takes to be made, but keep in mind that Thomas Edison failed his way to inventing the light bulb. With each failure Edison chalked this up as a successful way NOT to make a light bulb!

Many people suffer from "paralysis of analysis" where they get side tracked into investigating every opportunity to find that "perfect" one and therefore they never take any further action. These kinds of people are always learning and never implementing—just educated lame ducks. Avoid them.

4. **They have the entrepreneurial sprit**. This raises the question, "what makes a good entrepreneur?" What separates those who want to work for themselves instead of working for another company? Here are some common traits of the entrepreneur:

    -   Risk takers
    -   Self-starters
    -   Good leaders
    -   Not afraid of responsibility
    -   Very organized
    -   In for the long haul
    -   Competitive
    -   Creative
    -   Good planners
    -   Comfortable living without the structure of a regular job.

    Your prospect may not have all the traits of an entrepreneur but if they have most of them, then you know that you are targeting the right crowd. And perhaps you have heard the saying that, "if you want anything done find a busy person". Intuitively, you'd think that this person wouldn't have enough time for your opportunity, but because they are busy shows they know how to cope with deadlines and are usually very organized. This means that your best distributors will be entrepreneurs who are already busy with success in other businesses.

5. **They love helping people**. It's no accident that some of the richest people in the world are also the most generous. Take the legendary John D.

Rockefeller for example. From his very first paycheck, Rockefeller tithed ten percent of his earnings to his church. As his wealth grew, so did his giving, primarily to educational and public health causes, but also for basic science and the arts. Over his lifetime he gave away approximately $550 million. Also, according to a 2004 *Forbes* magazine article, Bill Gates gave away over $29 billion to charities from the year 2000 and onwards.

Successful network marketers are also generous with their time and talents and primarily want to help people rather than simply make themselves rich. Money comes as a by-product of helping people. It was Zig Ziglar who said, "You can get everything in life you want if you will just help enough people get what they want."

The bottom line is that you want to target your marketing towards people with the above characteristics rather than throwing mud against the wall and hoping that some will stick. It makes sense to fish where the fish are biting. And fish in the lake where the fish that will nourish you live—no use looking for catfish when you are trying to catch trout!

Practically, in the online world you would want to:

- Target your PPC keywords towards people who are searching for information on starting a home business or want to make more money from home (i.e. Other network marketers)

- Advertise on a website that caters to entrepreneurs and self-starters.

- Join forums that discuss network marketing and you'll attract like-minded people

- Create marketing messages that filter the "tire-kickers" and are geared towards ambitious people, people that take action.

Understanding who your target market is, and learning to market to them will give you an edge over all other network marketers. This basic principle of marketing is often overlooked and could save you a lot of time and money!

As one marketer said, "Give me a barrel full of fish to fish from, rather than having to throw a line out in the ocean!"

9

Overcoming Buyer Resistance

Those who are brave enough to camp in the wild carry with them a survival kit. This kit may contain a compass, first aid items, bug spray, a Swiss army knife and other items that would help them out of any anticipated challenges or emergencies. It's the same way for the marketer or sales person; they have to be prepared for the objections that surface during the "interview" stage with the prospect. A major part of selling is answering buyer's objections and the more prepared, the better you'll be able to handle them when they arise.

Rather than running away from objections, skilled sales people love to hear customer objections because they indicate that the prospect is seriously thinking about making the purchase. Just think, why make a big deal about something you are not at all interested in? If you have zero interest then you'd just walk away rather than take time to ask questions.

Below we'll look at the most common categories of buyer resistance (objections) and propose how you can answer each of these questions. Here are the obstacles you must overcome:

1. Fear—"I'm not like you, I can't do this"

2. Credibility—"Why should I listen to you"

3. Self-absorption—"What's in it for me?"

4. Skepticism—"Seems to good to be true"

5. Procrastination—"Let me think about it"

6. Fear of taking risks—"What if I doesn't work or I don't like it?"

7. Finances—"I don't think I have the money right now"

Let's take each objection one by one and discuss how you can overcome it so your prospect will sign up with your opportunity.

1. Fear—"I'm Not Like You, I Can't Do This"

One of the best and most subtle ways to overcome this one is with a personal story that leads the prospect to immediately identify with you. Apart from the pull of the product, most network marketing businesses are marketed as a way to add another stream of income. You can therefore include in your sales material a story (or *your* story, whichever is better) of an average person just like your prospect who was struggling and tried several different ways to increase their cash flow until finally they had a breakthrough when they tried your opportunity. In other words, do your best to relate to your prospect and give them assurance that you know where they are coming from.

Stories can have several functions in direct selling but one of its greatest appeals is the indirect nature of how it creates conviction. If I tell you my personal story then you cannot accuse me of trying to convince you of anything—it's just my story. In a way, every testimonial about your product is also a personal success story with the product and serves a similar function. Most people don't realize that some of the best salesmen have been the greatest story tellers! (Just make sure you tell TRUE stories)

Look at the example below to see how the writer used his own story to sell a network marketing opportunity:

Dear Friend,

I'm Doug Vass and I've often dreamt of the perfect network marketing situation: free-flowing money, an executive team I could be proud of, the very greatest product to sell and a sleek, easy going marketing plan to pull it all together and make it run without the need for time, tools, or know-how.

Well, up until now, if 'experience' is what you get when you don't get what you want, let's just say I've experienced it all.

I've read the books ...

Gone to more dreary hotel meetings than Hilton ...

Attended calls, meetings, events ...

Stuck a fork in my goal cards after watching them turn brown over time

... and at long last ...

Discovered how to finally and forever succeed ...

No. I did everything I was told to do and I did it to the letter.

Note how the writer weaves into his story the many different methods he had tried before he reveals his "secret method", because he knows that his target audience would have tried and been disappointed with those methods as well!

2. Credibility—"Why Should I Listen To You Anyway?"

This question has to do with your credibility or authority in the filed and why the prospect should bother to listen to you. Your prospects are wondering why they should believe you. Here is where you have to give all the reasons why you can be trusted.

There several ways you can showcase your credibility in the field. These include:

- Talking about the prestigious companies you have done business with and the success you had before. The psychology here is that if these "big wigs" can trust you then this prospect can as well.

- Showing the awards or recognition you have received within your field. You may want to show the downlines you have grown in other companies, the titles and levels you have achieved within the industry and certificates awarded.

- How long you have been doing this business and your experience in the field.

- Books or articles you have written and conferences you have spoken at or TV shows you have appeared on. *"As seen on TV"* is still a great advertising line.

- The financial success and lifestyle that your business affords you.

- What other people have said about you, especially other experts in the same field and newspaper write-ups.

If you position yourself in a place of authority in your field then you'll get more attention. This is why article marketing works so well because you are showing your expertise and building credibility for yourself. Many professionals have published a book to distinguish themselves from their competition. If you wrote the book on the subject then you must know what you are saying!

Warning: Be careful not to brag. No one likes someone who is high on themselves. Establish your credibility with tactfulness.

3. Self Absorption—"What's In It For Me?"

Prospects are always thinking about themselves. They don't care if you have the best product in the world or are part of the greatest opportunity. They need to know how your product or business opportunity is going to meet their needs. Asking your prospect questions and listening attentively to them will give you clues as to what they are looking for.

Once you have determined what it is that they are looking for then make sure to show how your opportunity will give them exactly that.

4. Skepticism—"Sounds too good to be true"

This is one of the biggest hurdles to overcome within the network marketing industry. The reason is because many network marketers make promises of millions of dollars for little or no work and this has scarred the reputation of the industry. People come in with high expectations and soon disappear after the millions don't come flowing in as promised.

Has this industry produced millionaires? Yes! Can you make a ton of money? Yes! Do you need a lot of money to start a network marketing business? No! So, what is the problem with making these promises?

What is true and what is BELIEVABLE could be night and day apart. In other words, the truth is not always believable, and therefore when these big promises are made people naturally shy away because they think it is just too good to be true.

Many people who could be benefiting from such opportunities cannot wrap their minds around a million-dollar per year income. Most people can't even think about making $10,000 per month! If you talk to the self-made millionaires in this industry and ask them if they thought they would ever become a millionaire, they would say no. As their businesses grew so did their expectations.

Making these huge promises may seem like HYPE to most prospects even though they may be true!

The savvy marketer must then work with the prospect where they are and build from there. Instead of promising millions, promise a couple thousand per month—anything that seems attainable for the prospect.

Testimonials are "social proof" and are one of the most effective ways to overcome this objection. The prospect is more likely to believe what others say about your opportunity than what you have to say, for obvious reasons. Sometimes a complete ad can be made up of just one long testimonial.

Testimonials that work best are written in the words and voice of the people who give them and show measurable results they received from using the product or joining the opportunity. One of the best types of testimonial is a "before and after" case study commonly used to advertise weight-loss and cosmetic products.

Read through the testimonial below:

> *"I can't say enough about the training and capabilites of the Zfreedom team. I tried pay per click advertising prior to the training by Dave Vass and it cost me a lot with little results. Now I have more qualified Zrii leads than I can respond to and the tactics you taught makes it so affordable I can keep doing it as long as I want to and share with my leaders, too. Dave's training made it so simple. I have put dozens of ad-groups up on Google and am tracking click and conversion rates on all of them with ease using the Ad Tracking in my OGW back-office. Keep up the good work and thanks again!—Rick S."*

Note that this testimonial is in the words of Rick even with the spelling errors! Why leave these errors in? These errors make the testimonial more home-grown, down-to-earth and believable. The more polished a testimonial is, often the less believable it will seem.

If a family of 10 invited you over for lunch and the floor was clean as a hospital operating room, you'd immediately think that they cleaned up for your visit and this is not the way a home with eight kids looks like all the time. Obviously they are trying to make an impression on you!

It's the same with a testimonial—if the person speaks in all superlatives and everything is presented as being perfect then you know something must be wrong.

WARNING: Testimonials are great selling tools but it is both foolish and unethical to give false or made-up testimonials. Some unethical marketers do this and that is why it's best to give the full details (i.e. name, address, picture, etc,) of the person giving the testimonials to make it more believable.

5. <u>Procrastination—"Let Me Think About It"</u>

This may first appear as a legitimate objection but it's most often a call for more information or to cover some other underlying objection. The prospect may just want to appear polite, so instead of saying "no" they say, "I need more time to make a decision."

The problem here is that the prospect seldom ever thinks about it again, not because they lied, but because some other competing idea or opportunity took her attention away from yours. In a majority of cases there seems to be no urgency about making a decision right away.

Your job therefore is to create urgency to the offer and you can do this in several different ways:

- **Offer premiums or bonuses**. Often your primary offer may not be strong enough to get the prospect over the line and into your camp. This is why you should offer bonuses to those who act within a certain time frame. CrackerJack® has been using this "trick" for ages to sell their boxes of sweetened popcorn to kids who can't wait to see what bonus awaits at the bottom of the box. Most children are more exicted about the surprise gift inside than the candy popcorn itself.

- **Show limited availability**. Your offer may only be good for a short period of time and the "ground-floor" positions may be going fast. Tell your prospects that positions are filling up fast and they could lose out if they don't act fast.

- **Prize break for those who respond right away**. You can offer a discount for those who respond within a certain period time after receiving your offer. This way the prospects know that they would lose the discount if they don't decide right away.

- **Give a deadline**. This can be used in combination with other techniques but giving a deadline can prove very effective, especially if in the follow up you keep mentioning a countdown to the deadline.

- **Make it easy to respond**. Putting your prospects through a number of hoops before they can sign up for your opportunity, will result in a drop in response to your offer. There are some websites that make it almost impossible to buy from because the webmaster practically hides the order link or order information. Making responding easy includes adding as many response channels as possible, such as phone, fax, online, snail mail and email.

6. Afraid of Risk—"What If It Doesn't Work Or I Don't Like It?"

This is a legitimate fear because we have all bought things that we were disappointed in afterwards and felt foolish about being duped. A simple money-back guarantee would calm this fear and the stronger the guarantee the higher the response to your offer will be.

A 30-day money-back guarantee is usually part of legal protocol for companies and adds legitimacy to your offer. The longer your guarantee period is, the more sales you'll get and the less likely your prospect will back away from your offer.

This is a good place where you can also address after-purchase concerns, such as how you would continue to support the customer even **after** the purchase. This contributes greatly to customer retention and future referral possibilities.

7. Finances—"I Don't Think I have The Money Right Now"

This is simply another way of the prospect saying, "*I don't think that the money that you are asking for is equivalent to the value that I'm getting from your product.*" When you are met with this objection it either means that you have not spelled out the value of your product enough or the prospect doesn't see how they can benefit from the offer.

This objection gives you opportunity to show the "real value" of your product. You have to show all the benefits the prospect receives and not get hung up on the features of your product. It's not enough to show how much money someone can make without showing what that person can do with the money. What we actually want are the comforts and security that money provides.

Important: Always show the final consequences of the features that your opportunity provides. For example, people don't buy nutritional supplements; they buy the concept of being a healthier family. People don't buy big screen TV's but entertainment and time spent with friends! Get past the feature to show the prospect the benefit they will receive. In other words, always meet your prospects wants and needs.

Meet Them Where They Are

So far we have looked at possible objections that your prospects might have and how it is very important to have a good answer. The only downside to these methods is that they could place you in direct opposition to the prospect. If you're not careful you can become involved in a tug-of-war where somebody will win and the other will lose. A win-lose situation is immediately set up from which somebody will walk away a "loser".

What if you learned to side with your prospect instead of trying to argue their position down? In this way, you become a facilitator to the prospect rather than the slick salesman trying to win the sale. Of course, this strategy can be misused as in the case of the slick car salesperson that pretends to argue with his supervisor in order to get you that big discount. He sets up a "we against them" situation and he becomes your friend who is trying to get you the deal. (At least that is what you're led to believe!)

A more legitimate and ethical way to use this strategy is to use the negative emotions that the person may have towards your product or industry as a launching pad towards closing the sale.

Let's consider how this can be done for a weight-loss product. You'll understand why I chose this industry in a minute.

For many years marketers have been making claims for their weight-loss products and many people have tried solutions from pills, to diets, to other various concoctions with little result. Because there are so many companies making claims about their products for such a long time people have become very skeptical about new products that come on the market.

What the savvy advertiser can do is tap into this negative emotion and attitude towards these products by stating up front the fact that most diet plans don't work or are too difficult to maintain. They could also state the common problems before making any claims about their product.

This way, the advertiser puts himself in their prospect's shoes so to speak by showing the prospect that he understands their pain. This opens the door to show how your product can be the solution to their problems. Now, the prospect is ready and willing to listen.

This is common with the MLM industry because so many claims have been made and many people have either been burnt or tried and have failed. Due to this high failure rate you'll most likely get a cold shoulder towards your opportunity.

Instead of being afraid of this reaction, agree as much as possible with your prospect and then move from the "common ground" to showing how your product or opportunity is different than the rest. A great approach is a method from sales guru, Tom Hopkins. He uses a process called, "Feel, felt, found". *"Mr. Prospect, I understand how you feel. I felt the same way you did about MLM opportunities. However, what I have found is that MLM is hailed as the real estate of the 21st century by many prominent business people."*

This approach will differentiate your marketing from 99% of other mlm'ers who are all making huge promises that people easily dismiss as hype. Just like the weight-loss product we talked about earlier, this type of an approach typically gets dismissed because it doesn't stand out from the crowd.

Objections Are Not Always A Bad Sign

Customer objections are a good sign that they are interested in your opportunity because they would simply "blow you off" if they were not interested. You will want to know what the common objections are and then answer these questions that are in the prospect's mind even BEFORE they are raised. One way of doing this is to raise the objection yourself and then answer the questions. This allows you to "take away" the objection before it even surfaces.

Here are just a few examples:

Prospect's Thoughts: "I know that a lot of people have been burnt in the pass by unscrupulous pyramid schemes and how do I know you are any different?"

Answer: "There are a lot of schemes out there and people have to be very careful about where they put their money. But, I can assure you that I only do business with a legitimate company. Let me show you why we are different."

Prospect's Thoughts: "How can I squeeze in another 5-10 hours in my week to market my business? I'm already so busy."

Answer: "I know what it is like to be busy. But, in the end we always make time for what we really want. Couldn't you use the extra income so you don't have to be as busy? I know I am willing to sacrifice a little time and effort now for the long term benefit of spending more time with my family. Are you?"

In these instances you are reading the prospect's mind and answering the objections even before they raise them. If you are getting too many objections AFTER you have shared your sales presentation this could be a good indicator that your presentation needs some tweaking. You may not be able to eliminate every possible objection but as you get new ones, be sure to answer them in the sales process.

10

The Duplicity Of Duplication

The whole concept behind network marketing is nothing less than magical. If you've been around this industry for a little while and recall when you first learned about an MLM opportunity, you knew how simple and powerful the concept is. Even a grade-school child can do the math. You get 3 people who bring in 9 people who in turn recruits 27 and the numbers multiply along with your residual checks.

You looked at the presentation and added up the numbers for yourself and they all made sense. And to think that you can make all that money from just telling a few people about this new and exciting business.

Let's take a look at what this network marketing model looks like practically if everyone just focused on finding 3 leaders, people who are open-minded and willing to do what is necessary, who in turn find their 3 leaders.

1st month = 3
2nd month= 9
3rd month= 27
4th month= 81
5th month= 243
6th month= 729 ... Typical Income: Approx. $8000-$12000
7th month= 2187
8th month= 6561
9th month= 19683 ... Typical Income: Approx. $200,000+

On paper this looks great but it was not long before you came to realize that you had to talk to 100 people in order to get 2 or 3 and those who were closest to you, the very people you thought would just jump on this opportunity didn't.

What went wrong? Well, it's the simple fact that there's a certain duplicity to duplication—you can't really duplicate yourself except in the movies. Some people seem like naturals in this business and other people just don't do as well. In order to experience the full power of leverage—that's another common word—you have to create a marketing system that gives results that can be easily duplicated.

In other words, you need a marketing system that depends as little as possible on who is using it.

You can learn a lot of lessons from what doesn't work so we will briefly consider an example of this.

Hotel meetings are typically held by some company recruiting superstar who will come into town and show the other "common folks" how this business is done. This person is normally very charismatic and a very skilled speaker who can both entertain and get people pulling out their credit cards for a buying frenzy.

However, new distributors go away thinking that in order to succeed in network marketing they have to be able to do the same as this superstar. Of course, most people are afraid of public speaking so the duplication ends here. If your effort cannot be duplicated then the real power of the network marketing concept just got hijacked.

Another common strategy used is that of cold calling. This is where the new distributor is told to buy lead lists to call and call people from the phone book. But a lot of people can be intimidated about doing cold-calling and never get off to providing the same service to their downline and so the duplication ends.

The bottom line is that in order for duplication to take place, the system of marketing has to be as duplicable as possible so that it doesn't depend on the marketing skill of whoever is using it. For example, if you mail out packages with a DVD presentation of the opportunity then your success will depend on how persuasive the sales pitch is on the DVD and not who mailed out the package. The only limitation is that the cost of mailing packages can add up quickly and you are looking at a typical response rate of 2-3 sign-ups per 100 packages mailed out.

The few stars that shone within a network marketing company were those with prior business experience or who had been in the industry for a while and therefore had enough influence to move their entire downlines with them into a new company. Or maybe they had experience in advertising in national magazines and were willing to take the expense risk that a normal home business entrepreneur wouldn't take.

Whatever the situation may be, it wasn't a clear case of duplication. The reason you are reading this book right now is to better understand how you can become successful in this industry while avoiding the pit-falls of past marketing paradigms.

A common false expectation of many network marketers is that they will not have to learn anything new, or they won't have to place any real effort into the business in order to make it work. Any business that can place you in the income bracket of the top 1% in the world should require some effort, don't you think? But you don't want to be rowing with one oar and end up going around in circles, either.

Again, the ideal duplication marketing system will therefore be independent of who is using it—NOT dependent on personality—taking away the guess work and injecting more predictability into how effective the system will be.

People are not duplicable, but marketing systems are!

11

It's Not How Great Your Product Is

There are hundreds of great companies with great products that bite the dust each year. Guess what the common problem is? They don't know how to market, or get their message out to their target audience.

I'm not convinced that Coke™ is the best tasting drink but they do know how to market and, therefore, dominate the soda drink industry. The beverage industry is one of the hardest to break into because those who dominate really do so through effective, ongoing marketing campaigns. You'd think by this time Coke™ would relax their marketing efforts but on the contrary they continue to bring out new advertisements. They know that if they rest easy on their laurels, this gives opportunity for their competitors to move in.

The point is that you cannot depend on a great product or company to ensure marketing success. <u>If you don't advertise you die</u>. In his book *Ogilvy on Advertising*, mastermind advertiser Ogilvy shares this anonymous poem:

> *The codfish lays ten thousand eggs,*
> *The homely hen lays one.*
> *The codfish never cackles*
> *To tell you what she's done—*
> *And so we scorn the codfish*
> *While the humble hen we prize.*
> *It only goes to show you*
> *That it pays to advertise!*

In the same book, Ogilvy shares this anecdote:

"On a train journey to California, a friend asked Mr. Wigley why, with the loin share of the market, he continued to advertise chewing gum. 'How fast do you think this train is going?' asked Wigley. 'I would say about ninety miles an hour.' 'Well', said Wigley, 'do you suggest we unhitch the engine?'"

The point is clear, but how many new distributors with a great company and product never make a dime because they thought that people would beat a path to their door?

Perhaps you've watched *American Idol*, one of the most popular shows in the US. There is of course the good, the bad and the potential stars that eventually shine through weeks upon weeks of grueling judges' critiques and hoping that their fans would vote for them. The question is, "where were these stars before the show?" The show didn't give them their great voices but it did give them <u>exposure</u>. Yes, they found a chance to "cackle" and draw attention to their one egg, just like the hen.

Note again: the show did NOT give them their talents but just the opportunity to show the world. The lesson here is that even with a breakthrough product that everybody needs your business can still go under if you don't get the sales message in front of a targeted audience. <u>It really is a numbers game</u>.

<u>The Great Divide</u>

The great paradox of the MLM industry is that so many people fail at it and yet it has been so kind to others. Many ordinary people without super skills or education have become self-made millionaires through this industry. This begs the question, "what's the difference between these two groups?"

Human beings are complex creatures and any attempt to classify people into two different groups will always have its flaws. But I think it's safe to say that those who fail in this industry, apart from those cases where the companies failed the people either through inferior products or company management, did so because they forgot the "marketing" in network marketing.

Most people who come into this industry know very little about how to market a product. They depend on their uplines who may be just as ignorant. Some people make it through with sheer effort and what I would call the "economy of scales"—if you throw enough mud at the wall some will stick—but they could have been much more efficient if they knew the proper way to market their businesses.

People who join this industry come from all walks of life and unless they have some prior business experience it's likely that they will take marketing for granted or will be ignorant of how success hinges on effective advertising.

Why MLM Companies Stress Product Over Marketing

Let's take a brief look at the whole philosophy behind network marketing.

If you've ever visited a restaurant and recommended it to your friends then you helped advertise this business through word-of-mouth advertising. This happens to be one of the most effective means of advertising, promotion or marketing. And it is the method used by network marketing companies in order to advertise their products, except that in MLM you are paid to talk to others and convince them on how good the product or restaurant is.

A typical business spends up to fifty percent of the price of their goods on advertising and marketing expenses. If you were wondering why breakfast cereals are so expensive, being made from corn and sugar, just look at the pretty packaging! The cost of the box itself is almost half that of its content. The pretty four color boxes are really a big part of the advertising. The same cereal in a plain box would taste the same.

Instead of spending these advertising dollars with TV stations, radio and newspapers, the network marketing company shares this with its distributors in the form of commissions.

The distributor is paid what would traditionally go towards company advertising. This is the very reason why you cannot depend on the company to advertise for you and why most companies have very poor marketing systems set up for their distributors—that's what they are paying their distributors for!

MLM companies sink their dollars into product development which explains why most network marketing products are usually superior to similar products from traditional companies. If a MLM company tries to market a product that can be easily found in your local Wal-Mart, this would be a poor product choice and it's obvious that they'll fail. This is why you cannot depend on the company for marketing and usually need an independent marketing system that you can use to promote your products or service with.

There are many companies who will sell you a marketing package to help in your launch but you cannot depend on these tools because they are normally ineffective. A good example of this is where the company provides you with a replicated website that is not designed to sell. The company means well in providing this site but good intentions won't help you hit the high numbers.

The key point here is you need to develop a marketing system or join a group that has invested in a system and understand how to market, not just hype a product. This can mean the difference between success or failure for you as a distributor.

Being a network marketer, you only get paid when you are successful. Put another way, you only get commissions when you make the sale. This means that the company doesn't lose money on YOUR advertising but they do gain money when your advertising works. This doesn't mean that the company is not concerned about your success but you just need to make sure that you are as effective and efficient as possible when marketing your business.

The cold hard fact that you have to keep in mind as you work out your marketing plan is all risk for advertising is on you! Do your due diligence when choosing what team to be on.

12

A Good Marketing System Can Eliminate The Majority Of Rejection!

So far we have looked at the importance of effective marketing to your overall success in network marketing and the importance of having a system in place. We have even looked at the components that such a system should have if you are marketing using the internet which this book is all about. The remaining question is, "how do we put all the marketing pieces together in order to build a system that will work for you?"

First, let's take a look at what a typical traditional marketing plan would look like for doing network marketing:

- Define your personal goals and visualize yourself as reaching those goals and commit to this by writing it down.

- Make a list of 100 warm market leads, people with whom you share the opportunity, and then start with your family members and close friends.

- Be sure that you are using the products yourself and find ten customers who will enjoy them as well.

- Do 3-way calls with your upline sponsor until you are confident with the "sales pitch" to survive on your own.

In theory, this is a simple enough plan that should be easily duplicated except that over 90% of the people who follow this system fail! Why? The sign up rate is less than 5% for the most seasoned sales person. This means that over 95 people in a hundred will turn down the best sales person in the world—that's a 95% rejection rate. For the untrained beginner who cannot handle this rate of rejection, the only option is to drop out.

Now, to be fair to those who have gone down this path and failed, if they had continued with even a 2% success rate they could have been millionaires today. Most beginners don't know that professional mail order companies send out millions of letters each year and make a huge profit with a rejection rate of 97% or more! Within the direct marketing industry a success rate of even 1% could spell millions of dollars in profit depending on the profit margin of the product they sell.

But, for a beginner who has called on 25 family members and friends and got turned down, because they have unrealistic expectations about selling, they easily give up. As was mentioned earlier in this book, getting three who get nine, who get twenty seven, is a lot easier said than done.

A lot of energy goes into sifting through that 100 people before you can find your three who will even listen to you. Seasoned network marketers know that one good recruit can give you HUGE leverage but most people are not "battle hardened" enough to endure all that rejection.

The antidote for the number of "No's" has been to teach you mental tactics that will get you prepared. This involved listening to self-help tapes, correcting your attitude, and reading books on handling rejection. While there is a lot to say about the mental preparations to owning your own business and handling difficulties along the way, if you can eliminate the majority of rejection, then why not do it?

Simply put, if you can find a way to only deal with those people who are willing to do business with you then the battle is half won. Here is what such an ideal system would look like:

- You can significantly lower the likelihood that you'll hear a "No".

- The system sifts through the bulk of leads or prospects to find those who are highly interested.

- You talk only to those prospects that've gone through this pre-sifting process.

- You train new recruits to use the system to do the same.

You must agree that even if you hate selling you wouldn't find it difficult to sell to people who give you their contact information for you to call them. **In other words you'll become the pursued instead of the pursuer.**

In the traditional plan you gathered a long list of family and friends, called them and tried to sell them on the idea that you had the best opportunity in town. With this new marketing system people ask you to call them after they have read the benefits of your product or opportunity.

You are now in control of the process because you are letting them choose to come to you. Once they sign up, you can train them how to use the same system to repeat the whole process all over again.

Putting The Pieces Together

Up to this point we have looked at the theory of the system, now we are ready to look in more detail at how such a marketing system works.

If you've ever seen how prospectors pan for gold then you already have a conceptual map of how an effective marketing system works. The prospector uses a map to find a place where he expects to find gold and locates a stream. He then starts loading his pan with what seems to be pure muck. He carefully swirls the pan while the water from the stream takes away the lighter rocks and dirt and leaves the heavier gold nuggets behind. Some knowledge is required to at least tell the difference between real gold and fool's gold. This gold dust may seem small at first but they add up quickly in value. It's not everyday that a gold hunter will find a 54 pound nugget as was discovered in California but you can't find any gold if you don't look.

In the same way you want to use all the marketing avenues we have discussed so far to feed into your sifting pan and thereby discover the real nuggets. The diagram below shows how this is done:

[PPC] [Articles] [Email Marketing] [Newsletter] [Blog]

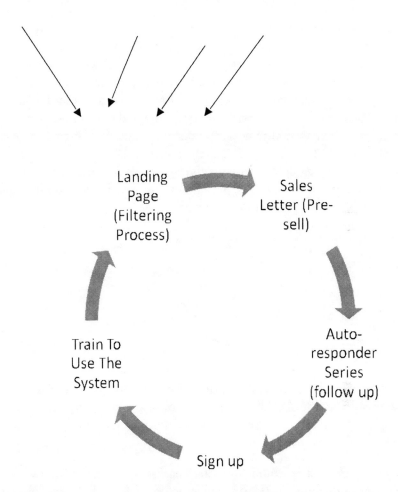

From the diagram above you can see that all the leads are fed into one central automated marketing system which takes care of the filtering, selling and follow up, saving you all the tedious work of sifting through hundreds of people. Thus, all of your prospects are highly targeted people who have willingly given you their contact information.

If the sifting and sorting is done without a system it then becomes the duty of the network marketer to do it. This can frustrate beginners and leave them disillusioned to say the least. Having a system do the sifting, sorting, and hard selling is perfect since it automates the whole the process.

It's like taping a sales presentation and then handing it out to people rather doing the same presentation one-prospect-at-a-time. You may have noticed that some of the most successful network marketers used teleconference calls or DVD mail outs to recruit new blood because it was/is a very economical way to use one's time. A similar strategy was also to use an 800-number with a recorded sales message and people would leave their names if they wanted more information. While these methods have their clear advantages over going it one-on-one, the internet is the perfect place for marketing systems because of the cheap technology that is available for following up on prospects through email. **By using an online marketing system you are doing one presentation to perhaps hundreds of people at the same time thereby creating leverage!**

In summary, an effective marketing system should:

- Teach You How To Generate Leads
- Capture Leads
- Automatically follow up with qualified leads
- Normalize the sales process through a direct response sales letter (sale NOT totally dependent on personality or skill).

The real power of the internet is that it can work for you 24/7/365 without requiring rest and does the "dirty" work for you at the same time. And compared to using the postal system to send out a package it's much cheaper, leaving you with more dollars to spend on advertising.

Just consider the cost of sending out 1,000 packages at $1 each. That's a total of $1,000 for mailing those packages to prospects out of which 25 may respond. If you sent out an email to those same 1,000 prospects even if only 25 responded, the cost for sending the email is practically zero! You can immediately see how much money you can save by using internet technology instead.

A Fair Warning

If you've ever called into a business only to be greeted by an automated message telling you which number to press to get which department, then you know how annoying technology can be at times. The problem with those long menus is that it always seems that the department you need is listed as the ninth option!

I read not to long ago how many companies are going back to a more personal touch by using live operators to answer the phone. The result is customers are finding this very refreshing. Technology is not always the solution to your problem, sometimes it can create additional problems.

There are some companies who rely too heavily on technology and never use the human touch at all. Such companies will promise that they will do all the work for you or show you how their marketing system will do all the work, but this never works as easily as they claim. At some point in the game people want to know that they are dealing with real flesh and blood and not just a computer.

What I'm presenting here is a system that does the sifting and "hard selling", but you still have to do some relationship building if you want to really hit the high numbers. Remember, network marketing is really relationship marketing.

13

Leads: To Buy Or Not To Buy?

According to the free online encyclopedia, Wikipedia, "**Lead generation** is a marketing term that refers to the creation or *generation* of prospective consumer interest or inquiry into a business' products or services. Often lead generation is associated with marketing activity targeted at generating sales opportunities for a company's sales force. *Therefore a lead is correctly described as information regarding or provided by a consumer that may be interested in making a purchase.* Whereas, *lead generation* is one of a myriad of activities that may produce that information and perceived interest."

That's quite a fancy way of saying, "finding potential customers or prospects". However you define "leads", your network marketing business cannot survive without them. The question is what are the different ways they are generated and should you ever buy them?

Methods Of Lead Generation

Lead generation is nothing new and not isolated to the network marketing industry. Companies in other industries have been using various means to build lists of interested clients for decades. The MLM industry has simply borrowed many of these techniques.

One of the traditional and most popular ways to generate leads is through sweepstakes. The company assumes that if you enter your name and contact information to win one of their products that you are interested in the product, so you become a lead within their marketing system.

A car dealership may run a sweepstake where the prize is a luxury vehicle. Your first reaction may be, "How can the company afford to give away a prize of such high value for free?", but this business knows that if they had to buy those names and contact information from a lead generation company they'd end up spending a lot more money than what it cost in giving away a free car.

Running sweepstakes is still the most popular way of generating leads as cheaply as possible. You can find thousands of websites offering things like free iPods or a chance to win a free vacation if you'll just enter your name and contact information.

This brings us to the question of lead quality. You can buy leads from lead vendors anywhere from just $0.01/lead to $25/lead. The price is often a measure of how difficult it is to gather the leads. And generally speaking, the more difficult it is to get the lead, the higher the prices will be.

Another factor that can determine lead prices, especially within the MLM industry, is if the leads are interviewed before they are passed on to you. It is assumed that this filtering process leaves you with a more qualified lead and therefore you have to pay for the extra work done by this company in weeding out the "tire kickers".

When you choose to buy leads from a company you expose yourself to a couple risks, the least of which is dealing with downright dishonest lead vendors. Many lead vendors will sell the same leads to more than one person and generate their leads in questionable ways. Often these leads come through "incentivized" channels where the lead is promised some gift for entering their information. These are the worst type of leads because they are not really interested in your business at all but simply want to get the gift.

The best form of lead generation guarantees the interest of the person in a particular product or opportunity by asking for their interest rather than "tricking" the person into giving their information. One of these "tricks" involves using pre-checked boxes requesting information while you are signing up for another product. This is a very popular method online where you'll fill in a form to download a free trial for a product and end up on a newsletter subscription list because you forgot to uncheck the subscription box! If leads are generated without the <u>intentional</u> act of the prospect giving you their contact information then you end up trying to court an uninterested or cold lead.

Most MLM lead generation companies would describe their leads as:

- **Real-Time Pre-Screened Leads**—these leads should be very "new" or recently acquired.

- **Pre-Screened Leads**—these leads have gone through some screening, but you should always understand how they were screened.

- **Surveyed Leads**—these leads have been asked a number of questions to better gauge their interest level.

- **Double Opt-in Leads**—these leads should have filled in an opt-in form and confirmed their email address by clicking on a link in an email automatically sent to them.

- **Autoresponder Leads**—these are lower quality leads, normally much cheaper than the above, intended to be loaded in an autoresponder so you can do your own filtering. Be very careful with these types of leads because of the likelihood of getting SPAM complaints.

Another category of leads comes from the distributor list of MLM companies who have gone out of business. The ethics of selling these names is questionable because when these distributors signed up with the company they had no intention or knowledge that their information would be sold. This could be a direct violation of the Privacy Act. Plus, you'll find that these leads are sold several times over meaning that if you are not the earliest to contact them you can be dealing with a very angry lead.

However, these leads are sold with the idea that since they were already in an MLM program, it will require less effort to sell them on your particular opportunity. This reasoning is similar to companies who sell their customer list to other companies that offer related products. A company that manufactures golf balls may sell their list to a company who publishes a golf magazine.

If are going to buy leads, you should only buy re-directed leads. These are leads that are immediately sent to your sales presentation and put into your marketing funnel in real-time. They are not incentivized or sold to anyone else. Of course, they cost a little more money but are well worth it in the end.

The "Real" Cost of Leads

Even when the leads are "hot quality" leads you can expect only a certain percentage to buy into your offer, so your advertising cost must be offset by the new business these leads bring or you will lose money fast!

For example, let's say that you bought 100 leads at a modest $5 per lead, so that's $500 from your advertising budget. You then contact those leads (which can take more than a couple hours out of your time) and a whopping 5 decide to sign up with you. Your cost per acquisition of a new distributor is now $500/5 = $100!

Next, you have to calculate the average time that a distributor remains with you, in other words, the lifetime value of that customer. If this is 6 months and you make a commission of $10 from each customer then you're looking at (6 x $10) = $60 per new distributor. Of course, within this timeframe, the new distributor can also recruit new members to your second level but we'll leave it at the first level for simplicity.

Now you have a clearer picture of the health of your business since each new distributor cost you $100 but you only make $60, leaving you with a loss of $40 or 40%! That is why it is very important to join a company with a good fast start bonus program where you get a really high commission upfront. The better the upfront commission, the more you can afford to spend per prospect. Just by doing this simple arithmetic, you can easily find out if the price you are paying per prospect is within reason.

The "Ideal" Leads

Hopefully, you can see why it is better to generate your own leads rather than depending on another company to do this for you. When you generate your own leads you have several advantages:

- You know where the leads originate, the advertisement they responded to, and thus how to best follow up with them.

- You can sometimes generate your own leads at a lower cost. Consider that the lead vendor is making a profit when they sell you leads. That means that lead vendors get their leads for less than they sell them to you for.

- You don't have to share your leads with anyone else. You have exclusive rights to them.

- If you happen to get a SPAM complaint then you'll have the immediate evidence that they opted in at your website rather than having to go back to the lead vendor for this evidence.

It shouldn't be hard to see that your network marketing business is really a lead generation business as fresh new leads are the lifeblood of your business. What-

<u>ever marketing plan you use it must be efficient in generating leads or it's not</u> <u>really a marketing plan</u>. Simply put, if you are not generating new leads for your business you are not doing the business anymore.

An ideal lead would be someone who is actively looking for your business opportunity. The question is; where do you find these people? You can find them on business forums, in your neighborhood, among your article readers and also searching for you in the search engines.

This is what makes pay-per-click (PPC) ads so effective because you are finding people at the time when their interest is highest. You can target a specific audience just by bidding on certain keywords or keyword phrases that are relevant to your target market. When your potential prospect searches for these keywords, your ad comes up. And the best part is you only pay when they click on it! Other types of advertisements can be viewed as intrusive, but pay-per-click ads are relevant to what your prospect is looking for.

Try to join a team in your network marketing company that understands how to apply various advertising methods to your business. They should be able to teach you PPC advertising, article marketing, blogging, banner advertising, contextual ads, etc. That way you can learn to generate your very own high quality prospects.

14

A Look Under The Hood

We have already been looking at the broad picture of what makes up an internet marketing system and now it's time to look under the hood of such a system and see why it works like a charm.

This system uses the strategies of direct marketing. Direct marketing refers to a method of advertising that sends marketing messages directly to the consumer with the intention to illicit a response that can be easily tracked. If you ever received a letter in the mail encouraging you to sign up for a credit card or any other "junk mail" then you already know how direct marketing works. One of the big advantages of this style of marketing is the accountability involved.

Just for comparison, let's look at another style of marketing for a moment—that of brand marketing. In this style of marketing there is no "call to action", only that the prospect will develop a positive impression of the company's product so that when they are ready to make the purchase they will hopefully choose that brand.

A brand is supposed to distinguish a product or service from its competitive offerings. For example, the Ford Motor Company tries to sell their brand as "tough", so you'll think of Ford Trucks as tough vehicles.

The big downfall of this type of advertising, apart from the tremendous cost, is that it is difficult to measure success. There is no way of tracking quantifiable data to determine whether or not the branding campaign worked. A company who spends one million dollars on a Super Bowl Sunday ad has no way of knowing the ads true effectiveness. I'm sure you would agree that the small business owner cannot afford such luxury.

One of the biggest advantages of direct marketing is that <u>you have a way of accounting for every single advertising dollar that you spend.</u> You know almost right away how much money it took to directly produce a profit. So if you invested $1,000 in your advertising and made $1,500 you know that you pulled in 50% profit.

OK, here we go …

Landing Page or Lead Capture Page

Perhaps you've heard the saying that all roads lead to Rome. Well, you'll recall from the diagram in the previous chapter that all the traffic from our marketing efforts is fed into the landing page. The landing page is the gateway into our marketing pan where we are looking for gold—prospects that will join our business or organization.

You'll notice that all the strategies and advertising methods that feed the lead capture pages (LCP) are like an open invitation to all who want to own a home business or make more money—very general indeed. This is the open invitation to view our company to see if they are interested in joining. However, the LCP must now ask for another level of commitment to show how serious they are by giving up their email addresses in exchange for more information.

For an effective LCP it's expected that upwards of 10-12% will give their contact information and therefore enter the marketing system at the first level.

These lead capture pages should be written by a professional copywriter who has studied how to write persuasive copy that moves people to take action. You'd be surprised to know how many MLM companies don't even consult a marketing expert or copywriter and attempt to write the copy themselves. This is a big mistake.

The anatomy of a well-crafted LCP starts with a strong and compelling headline, is often written in the form of a personal letter which gives some strong benefits for requesting more information and asks for the simple action of sending for more information.

If you've seen any TV commercials that sell expensive equipment, you'll notice that instead of going for the direct sale they ask the viewer to request a free CD or DVD, or brochure. These materials, which would be sent in the mail, are the real sales material that will try and persuade you to purchase the advertised offer. If the advertiser was to tell you the price right there in the TV ad within the 60 seconds or so for the commercial, you would not have enough information to make such an expensive purchasing decision.

Because the prospect receives the sale material in the mail, the advertiser can continue to follow up on this contact if a purchase is not made right away. Most importantly, the company now has a lead that they can advertise to over and over again.

In summary, the main purpose of the landing page is to get the visitor's contact information. After the visitor enters their name and email address then they are automatically forwarded to the main sales page.

Main Sales Letter Page

The main sales letter is similar to the lead capture page but with a lot more details. Along with a strong headline and sub headlines, there are:

- Testimonials of customers who found success with the product
- Benefits of using the product and joining the opportunity
- Company profile that lends credibility to the opportunity
- A statement of guarantee where applicable
- "Call to action" to join or buy the product
- Frictionless sign up process

The main sales letter is a key component to persuading the prospect to take action right away. This letter is the <u>heart of the system</u> in the sense that it carries the weight of persuading the prospect to take the decisive step. This letter should be written by a professional copywriter, which may seem expensive at first but if well-written can pay for itself within a short period of time.

Follow Up Emails

This is one of the most crucial steps in the marketing process and can be the difference between success and failure. Market researchers tell us that a typical prospect needs to be exposed to a marketing message 7-10 times before they take action. People live busy lives and may intend to get around to signing up with you someday but they may have forgotten where they saw your ad or never bookmarked the website so the prospect is lost forever. If you have the email address of that prospect then you have their permission to contact them until you run out of messages or they decide to unsubscribe.

The main focus of each auto-responder email is to close the sale by directing the prospect back to the main sales letter. These emails are usually brief and to the point, with the link to the sales letter all throughout the message.

The auto-responder service that sends out these messages for you at a predetermined interval will automatically remove the prospect from the series as soon as they sign up. This prevents your prospect from receiving more unnecessary autoresponder messages.

Another great aspect about using an autoresponder service is that the prospect generally doesn't know that the emails are sent out by an automated system, especially since the email is customized with the business owner's name.

Tracking System

Earlier we mentioned that it was important to be able to measure the results that you are getting from your marketing efforts. You should be able to trace exactly where your sales are coming from to know which advertisements are working. The ability to track your advertisements is a feature that all effective marketing systems should have. The process of tracking is simple. A tracking code (or "promo code") is usually added to the end of the url that you are using for a specific advertisement. This tracking code allows you to distinguish where your prospects are coming from.

This can best be illustrated by using an example. Let's say that we have five different advertising channels which are feeding our lead capture pages with visitors. We can "tag" each link used to respond to these ads with a unique identifier such as:

- http://www.domain.com/promo1
- http://www.domain.com/promo2
- http://www.domain.com/promo3
- http://www.domain.com/promo4
- http://www.domain.com/promo5

Every time someone comes to the LCP, they would be identified by the "promo code" used and when they sign up, they would be tracked right back to the source of the advertisement. This way you can determine where your customers are coming from and which advertising channels are working best.

Tracking is not new to direct marketing. If you ever noticed a response card for an advertisement in a magazine with an address such as:

ACME Company

Dept. Z2

P. O. Box 1234, Any Town, USA

The "Dept Z2" is actually the tracking that shows which magazine you read or the location you were responding from. In other words, there is no "Dept Z2"; it's just a way of identifying the source of the response.

If you want to make every advertising dollar account for itself then you must have a tracking system to measure results.

Leads and Contact Management

If good quality leads are the lifeblood of your business, then an efficient contact management system critical. You will find that as your business grows so will the number of names, phone numbers and email addresses. This makes it difficult to monitor the follow-up process. If you were dealing with just 20 names then a single spreadsheet would satisfy your needs but as your organization grows in the thousands you can quickly outgrow that sheet.

Any marketing system should therefore have a contact management system that allows you to keep track of the necessary statistics on your prospects:

- What advertisement did they respond to?
- How many times have they opened up the emails?
- What is their interest level?
- When did they sign up?
- When was the last time you spoke to them on the phone or contacted them by email?

… And the list goes on.

One of the most important parts of the contact database is to be able to contact your distributors on a regular basis so you can do training, send new information or just share a story to motivate your downline.

Before the internet, the best you could have done was send post cards or hold teleconference calls on a regular basis. The advent of auto-responder technology and mass mailing has now enabled these tasks to be preformed more efficiently and for a whole lot cheaper. With just one click of a button you can send an email message to all the names on your list. Of course, you will want to be able to personalize each email message that goes out and be able to track how many people actually open those emails. All this information will go a long way in helping to fine tune your marketing.

15

Test! Test! Test!

The current land speed record is currently held by a British RAF pilot, Andy Green, using the ThrustSSC, a twin turbofan jet-powered car which has achieved 763 mph (slightly under 1228 km/h) over one mile, breaking the sound barrier. This record was set in the Black Rock Desert in Nevada, USA, on 15 October 1997. Just compare this to one hundred years before when the record was just under 40 mph (63 km/h).

You can hardly call Andy Green's car engine a "motor" since it was powered by two Rolls Royce jet engines. Engines have come a long way over the past century due to advanced testing and technology. I don't know how long Andy's record will last but you can bet that there are people working hard to beat this record. You know what they say, "records are made to be broken".

No successful marketing system can remain static. It must always be improving, even when you are making a profit. No MLM'er can reach a place where they just stop recruiting (at least at the beginning phase of your business) or they will eventually lose their business growth. In order to increase the efficiency of any marketing system you need to keep track of how your ads are doing and make incremental changes towards increasing the conversion rate.

You Have To Start Somewhere

A Chinese proverb says that the journey of a thousand miles begins with a single step. When you begin a marketing campaign, if you were to wait until you got everything perfectly right then you'd never start. Some people get paralyzed simply because they are afraid to be wrong.

We mentioned before that direct marketers get pretty excited when just 3 in 100 respond to their offer. Why? If you know your conversion rate then you can set your advertising campaign accordingly. The best marketing piece would then become the standard or the control against which they would try to improve or beat the control.

The Scientific Process of Testing

In any kind of scientific testing you need a control or a standard against which you can measure the results. In clinical trials for example, a few patients would be given a placebo—usually a sugar pill—while the others would be given the real drug they are testing. The theory is that the difference between those who were administered the "real thing" and those who got the placebo should be an accurate gauge of the effect of the drug. If the company has variations of the same drug, they should be able to accurately test which one out performs the rest.

In the same way you have to make changes in your marketing pieces to try and improve your results. The majority of marketers, once they make money, never make any changes to their advertising and are often too lazy to do any testing. Testing is not the most exciting part of marketing but it is a necessary evil.

As an example of how this process works let us consider how we can improve a lead capture page (LCP).

The first thing we have to decide is what parameters to change. We may want to test a new headline, a different style font, or the color of the background of the web page. The important rule we must never break is to only change ONE parameter at any given time. This means that if we are testing a new headline then we must compare the results we get from the new headline to the old headline.

To make this test meaningful we have to treat each page the same way except that the only difference would be the headlines. We must send each page the same amount of traffic from the same source (e.g. PPC ad) for about the same period of time. Because it wouldn't be feasible to send the same prospects to the different pages, we can rotate the pages so that every other visitor to the page sees one version of the headlines. This type of testing is called an "A/B split testing". Direct mail marketers have been doing this style of testing for many years.

For those who see this test an unscientific we have to admit that we cannot control every aspect of this test but statistically speaking if we send enough traffic to these two LCP versions then it should give us a fair idea about which headline works the best.

So if our control page got an opt-in rate of 10% and the new headline performed at 15% then we can say that the second headline was the winner. The next step is to try and improve on this headline where our new winner would now become the control.

There is software sold for hundreds of dollars that will allow you to test more than one parameter at a time. This software uses very complicated mathematical formulas to calculate your winner. But carrying out a simple A/B split test can be just as effective. The vast majority of marketers do not test at all which means that they leave a lot of money on the table. Remember, testing does not just apply to your LCP but also to your PPC ads and any other type of ads you might be doing.

Quality Traffic Is Gold But It's Not Everything!

Once you choose to market your business online then traffic becomes a huge concern. Some businesses think that by just having a website they'll suddenly get people beating a path to their virtual doors and they'll be in profit over night. Only if life was that easy! We have already considered some ways to get more traffic in an earlier chapter. You can basically try and get free traffic (article marketing) or buy it (PPC ads); there are whole courses on how to get more traffic to your website but this is not our major concern here.

What we want to consider in this section is, "Should you invest your money in getting more traffic or improving the converting power of your websites or PPC ads?" Most people choose to spend money on the former and don't realize the leverage of spending money on the latter.

You will be surprised to know what one little change to your sales copy can do to increase your conversion rate. This is why many companies pay huge money to marketing consultants who make changes to their websites.

Let's take a typical situation. Imagine that your website is achieving a 2% conversion rate. This means that for every 1,000 visitors you are making 20 sales. If your product cost $50 then that's (20 X $50) = $1,000 per 1,000 visitors or $1 per visitor—not bad.

However, let's say that these are visitors from your Pay-Per-Click campaign and you are paying 25 cents per visitor. That is a total cost of $250 per 1,000 visitors. So your real net profit is ($1,000 - $250) = $750 or $0.75 per visitor.

Now let's look at two ways you may attempt to increase your sales. You can either buy more traffic or tweak your website so you increase your conversion rate to 3%.

Let's take each scenario and see what happens. We have not placed a time factor on this so we will use your weekly traffic. If you buy 2,000 extra clicks via PPC advertising then you will increase your net profit and it might look something like this—spent $500, made $1,500. You are now netting $1,000 instead of $750 i.e. 33% increase—great.

But, what would happen if, instead of buying more traffic, we could tweak our conversion from 2% to 3%. We pay $1,000 for 1,000 visitors, but now make 30 sales at $50 = $1,500! Our bottom line now reads the same $1,500 with the same investment in ads as before. That's a whopping 167% increase in profits! Compare that to a measly 33% and you will understand why it is so critical to invest time to optimize your website and other marketing pieces to reach their full potential.

One of the longest lasting and most successful direct marketing letters which brought in over $2 billion in sales was written by Martin Conroy for the Wall Street Journal. Just one great advertisement can make you rich!

Always Keep Testing

I've known this little saying from childhood: "Good, better, best; never let it rest till your good is better and your better is best." This is a perfect way to describe your marketing efforts. As soon as you become comfortable and complacency sets in, you'll lose your competitive advantage. When this happens your attrition rate will overtake your growth rate. The testing process will help keep you sharp and alert as to how your business is doing.

A general rule of thumb in network marketing is that you want to try to break even when advertising. Remember, even if you don't break even, that one good person could be worth tens of thousands of dollars. So don't be afraid to advertise and test. Even if it costs you a little more than you would have liked, you are still way ahead of most MLM'ers.

16

Phone Selling Skill Set

Although most good marketing systems are set up to use email as your primary means of initial contact you may find it necessary to talk to potential prospects on the phone. By doing so, you will increase your conversion rate. Network marketing is really relationship marketing, as was mentioned earlier, so this is not a good business to be in if you don't want to talk to people.

Does this mean that you cannot be successful if you're not using the phone? Of course not! Talking to your prospects will just ensure you have that much more success. Thus, it will be helpful to review some general tips when using the phone.

Who says that a successful salesperson has to be a "fast talker"? This is a common misconception when it comes to telephone and direct selling, but the opposite is true. It's the effective sales people who talk less and listen more that make the most sales. Active listening is a very important part of a network marketer's people skills. "Listen twice as much as you talk" is a good rule of thumb. For those who are dreading that they have to pitch the customer, this should come as a pleasant surprise.

Even though you think that you're sure of the prospect's needs, you have to listen because different individuals have totally different reasons why they purchase the same product or service. If you cannot ascertain the reason why your prospect wants to start a home business it's unlikely that you will win over the prospect.

The more apt you are to listen to your prospects, the more likely they'll tell you what they are looking for! Here are some quick tips to improve your listening and phone skills:

1. **Develop Great Rapport In The First 3 Seconds**

   Telemarketers know that they have only 3 seconds to establish great rapport. You don't have the advantage of using body language and gestures which make up a major part of our communication in face-to-face selling, so you have to use your voice and the spoken word effectively. A friendly personality and relaxed voice will help you not to sound too fake and so connect with your prospect.

2. **Just Stop Talking And Listen**

   This is the toughest part. As the salesperson, you think that you have all the information on the opportunity and so you need to educate the potential customer. The more passionate and enthusiastic you are about your business the more you'll have to pinch yourself at times to remind yourself to keep silent. If you just listen, you would hear the customer say, "These are my needs that I want you to satisfy." In other words, most people will end up telling you how to sell them!

3. **Learn To View Things From The Prospect's Position**

   It is easy to sympathize, but to place your self in the prospect's position—to empathize—is more challenging. Empathizing says that you understand the problems and challenges of your client and you are capable of viewing these problems from her position. Don't be afraid to affirm by saying, "I understand what you're saying", and mean it! For example, it's very likely that you'll talk to ex-MLM'ers who have had negative experiences with the industry. In such cases you'll have to first sooth their pain before you can apply your balm. Instead of being defensive, which will get you no where and only isolate the prospect more, you can even apologize and move on from there.

4. **Restate What The Client Tells You So That You Understand What They Are Communicating**

   This simple strategy makes the other person feel "heard". This is a common technique used by counselors and other such professionals, but works just as well in any human relationship. So if the prospect says, "Everybody seems to think that their opportunity is the best to come along, I don't know who to believe". You can reply by saying, "So you are concerned about choosing the right opportunity for you?" Here you've simply repeated the same statement idea but in your own words and the customer can confirm your understanding. Now we know that communication is really taking place.

5. **Try Not To Interrupt The Prospects While They Are Talking**

    Most people, instead of listening during a phone conversation, are eagerly processing what they are going to say next. When you interrupt your client in mid-sentence, you are actually saying that what he has to say is not as important as what *you* have to say. The irony here is that your client will then be anticipating you finishing your pitch, in order to complete their thought.

    Perhaps you have been on the other end of a telemarketer's call where you knew they were reading a script and have little concern if you are processing everything they said. You don't like when this happens to you, and you don't want to do this to your potential prospects.

6. **Ask A Lot Of Questions For Clarification But Not To Be Confrontational**

    Asking a lot of questions will draw out from the customer the benefits that she is hoping to gain from your business opportunity. Just be careful that your questions don't place the client in an awkward position or lead into an argument. Even when you recognize inconsistencies in the prospects reasoning, you don't want to embarrass them by making this flaw blatantly clear. A better approach will be to ask leading questions that will bring the prospect back to the place where you want them.

7. **Avoid Jumping To Unnecessary Conclusions And Learn To Listen Between The Lines**

    If you stereotype your prospect, you may find yourself jumping to conclusions that may circumvent your sales. Simply because the client is a single man in his 20's, doesn't mean that he is looking for a studio apartment. Here again, you have to be patient and skillful enough to allow the prospect to tell you what they need; instead of assuming the need because you perceive yourself to be the expert.

Many times you also have to listen to what is being said as much as to what is left unsaid. You have to "listen between the lines" and pick up on other signals such as tonal inflections and voice volume.

8. **Smile! You'll Be Surprised To See What This Does For Your Tone Of Voice**

Even if you're speaking to a prospect on the phone you should smile. Your smile will find itself expressed in your voice. Your voice communicates more than words; it also expresses mood. I'm sure that just after answering the phone you've been asked questions such as: "Are you in a hurry?", or "Is this a bad time?" Or hear statements such as: "You sound really excited!" "Well, you're really in a good mood today!"

Some marketers also find it helpful to stand and walk around just as if they were involved in an engaging conversation with someone in the room. Just standing and walking around pumps some extra adrenaline into your blood and the excitement comes through your voice.

Phone Follow Up

When you use a marketing system, you'll recruit most of your distributors once you've established a personal phone call. Due to the system, some might sign up automatically but that will be the exception NOT the rule. When they do sign up, a note of congratulations or simply reminding them that you are available to answer any questions, can go a long way to fostering a long business relationship.

17

Leadership Training

When you join a network marketing company you have to sign some sort of contract that gives you the right to be an independent distributor. The word "independent" not only shows your relationship to the primary company but indicates that you are in business for yourself. Congratulations!

However, the success of your business will depend on more than just you because, as we've mentioned several times now, you are involved in *relationship marketing*. The same skill set that will make you successful is the same skill set that you will want to duplicate in other distributors. You are a leader responsible for training others and it can be scary to think that you are involved in helping others succeed. If you are lazy and disorganized then you'll be discovered quite quickly and the attrition rate will show it.

There is a big difference between a leader and a manager. Warren Bennis puts this best when he wrote, "Many an institution is very well managed and very poorly led. It may excel in the ability to handle each day all the routine inputs yet it may never ask whether the routine should be done at all … *Leaders are people who do the right thing; managers are people who do things right.*"

Simply because you are going through the motions doesn't mean that you are a leader. Motion doesn't necessarily mean life. As a leader you must do what's right for your downline and get rid of the things that don't work. What you have to ask yourself isn't "Is this a good thing?" but "Is this *the right* thing?"

Leadership has to do with:

> 1. Who you are
> 2. How good you are at what you do

3. Living up to expectations

4. Accepting the consequences of your actions

1. **Who You Are—Character**

As a leader you must have the kind of character that will inspire other people to trust you to take them towards their goals. You have to prove yourself trustworthy and just faking it will not work for very long. This doesn't mean that you have to be perfect because nobody is, but you must have a <u>genuine interest</u> in the success of others; not just trying to advance yourself at another's expense. The whole philosophy of network marketing is based on personal growth through the development of others.

Character depends on a lot of factors such as your own belief system and spiritual development but you can't last long in this business if honesty and integrity are foreign words to you. You should need a lot of convincing on how a lack of character will eventually bring you down. *Enron* reminds us of that lesson.

2. **How Good You Are At What You Do—Competence**.

You should always be in learning mode. "How can I do this better?" is a question that should be foremost in your mind. Read books about the industry, learn new skills such as selling on the phone and develop your interpersonal skills. One thing you'll notice about successful network marketers is that they are always on a path of self-development. Even if they had little education before their new found wealth, the confidence that comes along with success places them in new company and they want to lean more and excel at what they do.

Other areas you'll want to continually grow in are:

• effective communication

• motivation

• thinking and planning strategically

• evaluating results

• fine-tuning the process and delegating tasks to skilled team members

3. **Living Up To Expectations**

   Apart from your skills you must also understand and know what is expected of you as a leader. You should read at least one book on leadership and study the qualities of a great leader. We are all leaders in one respect or the other. If you have a family, you lead others, and if you supervise other workers at your job, you are also a leader.

4. **Accepting Consequences For Your Actions**

   As a leader you will have to make decisions and they may not all turn out the way you anticipated. A real leader will admit mistakes when necessary and accept the consequences of those actions. Accepting consequences for your actions doesn't mean your always apologizing. Make decisions and stand behind them.

   The greatest moment of your leadership can be demonstrated in how you react when something goes wrong. Rudolph Giuliani, former mayor of New York City, made some very unpopular decision in his attempt to "clean up the city" but his leadership shone through after September 11.

What The Best Leaders Look Like

In his bestseller, *Good To Great*, Jim Collins relates the results of investigating some of the most successful companies in the world to find out why they excelled in their markets. He found six common characteristics shared by all these companies, the first of which he lists as Level 5 Leadership. In fact he defines his 5 levels of leaders as:

- **Level 1**—Highly capable individual who makes productive contributions through talent, knowledge, skills and good habits.

- **Level 2**—Contributing Team Member who contributes individual capabilities to the achievement of group objectives and works effectively with others in a group setting.

- **Level 3**—Competent Manager. Organizes people and resources toward the effective and efficient pursuit of predetermined objectives.

- **Level 4**—Effective Leader. Catalyzes commitment to and vigorous pursuit of a clear and compelling vision, stimulating higher performance standards.

- **Level 5**—Builds enduring greatness through a paradoxical blend of personal humility and professional will.

Collins and his research team came to the conclusion that those leaders who were at the top of the best companies were professionally driven and disciplined but they didn't strive to be in the limelight. In other words, they were *more* concerned about results than who got the credit for these results.

According to Collins, "Level 5 Leaders look out the window to attribute success to factors other than themselves. When things go poorly, however, they look in the mirror and blame themselves, taking full responsibility. The comparison CEO did almost the opposite—they looked in the mirror to take credit for success, but out of the window to assign blame for disappointing results"

The Practical Side Of MLM Leadership

In an earlier chapter we discussed that because a company who chooses network marketing as a distribution model doesn't invest in normal advertising, the distributors must be responsible for their own training. A company may provide some training material but 99 out of 100 times MLM companies' just plain suck at marketing.

The kind of marketing that will bring you real results are often discouraged by these companies because they are overly concerned about FTC regulations. Because the MLM industry is watched so carefully by the FTC, companies can become over cautious and in turn dampen the marketing efforts of the distributors.

A common leadership trap you'll have to be aware of is babysitting your downline. If your new distributors think that you are going to do everything for them then you are not really duplicating yourself and you'll suffer from burnout in a very short time. You want to find leaders who are self-motivated and want to learn as much as you want to teach. You will not find every new member on the same level but you can choose whom to invest your time and energy into.

Again, Collins also found that successful companies looked for the right people to hire rather than to mold people into what they wanted them to be. Be cautious that in your training you don't get stuck into rehabilitation mode, trying to get people motivated who don't want success for themselves. It's better to first find motivated people and show them that you have the vehicle to get them where they want to go. You'd be better off giving birth to a new distributor than trying to raise a dead one!

When you find leaders who may even be better than you, rather then trying to compete for the spotlight put them to work and facilitate their development. Always remember that their success is eventually your success. It is said that Henry Ford, the inventor of the automobile, wasn't highly educated but his brilliance was in surrounding himself with people smarter than himself.

Here are ten practical things you can do to ensure your leadership will be replicated in your downline organization:

1. **Develop a positive attitude towards the industry**. Often because of ignorance and poor logic, many people have unreasonable expectations about the network marketing industry. People often hold a higher standard for network marketing companies than they do other traditional businesses. For example, corporate America has more horror stories of dishonesty and fraud than the network marketing industry.

   Of course, there are good and bad companies in every sector but the network marketing industry is set up on a principle where people are paid according to what they are truly worth, not according to where they are in the corporate chain. The corporate setup is the real pyramid scheme where those at the top benefit enormously from those at the bottom!

2. **Create a culture of healthy expectation in your organization**. You set the tone for your organization and you must see the invisible. Many times new distributors are in business for themselves for the first time and are accustomed to a weekly paycheck determined by their companies. Now they are working for themselves and setting their own hours. It's a new experience but you can get them through the transition if you sell them on the possibilities.

3. **Lead by example**. Don't expect your downline to do what you won't do yourself. If you are not actively recruiting then you cannot expect them to recruit either. There are many leaders who think that the time has passed when they had to do the real hard work and they deserve to just sit on their throne and push around the commoners but this goes against the very philosophy of network marketing. If you want disciples you must be willing to wash feet.

4. **Reward innovative thinking**. Don't expect your downline to simply reflect what you are doing. If they try a new marketing method which works then you should reward them for their initiative. Many traditional type MLM'ers were negative towards the possibilities of building a viable downline using online marketing, but as they saw the results of new marketers they had to change their minds fast. Many more network marketers are waking up to the real potential of the internet.

5. **Don't covet the spotlight**. If you try and make a celebrity out of yourself then your organization will see themselves as your subjects and fans rather than business partners and could resent this. Remember what Collins said about Level 5 leaders? They are happy to stay in the background and allow others to enjoy the success. You are not on an ego trip to prove your worth but to help as many people as possible to accomplish their dreams.

6. **Be decisive**. It is often said that successful people make up their minds quickly and change their minds slowly. Nobody will respect an indecisive leader because they are never sure where you are in the game. All decisions won't be welcomed ones but you must be respected for knowing what you are about and following through with it.

7. **Be realistic and confront the facts**. There are times when you wish that things were different but you have to play the hand that you are dealt. If you spend your time daydreaming about how things were or how things could be then you are wasting your time and that of your downline members.

    You may wish that all your downline members were more internet savvy but if they are not then you can help them to develop these skills through training or focus on their other marketing strengths. The internet is NOT the only solution for marketing. There are times when your recruiting rate may slow down, such as during the Christmas holidays and summer. You simply confront these facts and work with them. Perhaps you can do more training during these slower months.

8. **Practice discipline**. If you are lackadaisical and slipshod in your approach to your business then you'll surely see poor results. Every business takes time and discipline if you want it to be successful. Don't be fooled by your own advertisement of a relaxed tourist sipping Hawaiian punch on the sunbathed beach while your commission checks stuff your

mailbox. Success follows hard work and this rule is only broken in gambling and the lottery for a lucky few.

9. **Build healthy relationships**. Your interpersonal skills will surely be needed as you are dealing with people not just technology. People will buy from you because they like YOU and not necessarily what you are selling. Marketers have known this for many years now and that's why they place beautiful people in their ads—they want you to associate likable people with their products. So bring out that warm personality and energize the people you work with because they will stay around longer if they like you. People are buying into you, not the product!

10. **Never quit.** You must never quit when the times get tough but this doesn't means that you have to keep hitting your head against a wall. There are times when quitting is the right thing to do and you may have to apologize to your down line. These times occur when a company goes belly-up. This is a success factor which is beyond your control. That's why it's so important to do your due diligence and investigate an opportunity before you invest so much time into promoting it. If you quit when things get rough, you'll soon find yourself skipping from opportunity to opportunity hoping to find the perfect company, which doesn't exist.

Zfreedom™

In closing, if everyone applied the principles of marketing as outlined in this book they would find themselves very successful. However, there are a few things that stop someone from actually doing all of this.

1. It can be very expensive creating your own marketing system

2. Most MLM companies don't have a marketing system in place complete with <u>effective</u> lead capture pages, sales letters, auto responders (all branded in your name), tracking tools, etc.

3. Most MLM companies don't have very good training on how to market your business effectively and efficiently.

If you find yourself in this position we have a solution for you. Zfreedom™ is a team started by Dave Vass, and Doug Vass who all have a passion to see others succeed in life. We chose Zrii as the network marketing company to be involved with because of the marketability of the company. With the Chopra name, Bill

Farley, Chris Gardner (Portrayed by Will Smith in The Pursuit of Happyness), Zrii is, in our estimation, the greatest opportunity ever seen in network marketing.

Zfreedom™ invites you to join us on a journey of a lifetime as we teach and coach others within Zrii so that they can succeed and watch their dreams become a reality. Zfreedom™ has created a comprehensive online marketing system for Zrii executives, complete with all the training you need in order to get a steady flow of prospects. It is not unusual for some people to get as many as 30-40 prospects a day!

The best part is that the founders of Zfreedom™ are ALL founding distributors of Zrii. That means that they have your best interest at heart. They are NOT just people trying to make a buck off of a marketing system. The whole reason they created the system is to give you an advantage and edge when building your Zrii business.

For more information about how you can become part of the Zfreedom™ team please visit http://Zfreedom.com. Or get in touch with the person you received this book from.

If you found this book to be useful and valuable then please pass it along to your friends and contacts. We could have charged top dollar for this book but instead chose to make it accessible to everyone. You never know who might benefit from reading it … in fact, everyone who has ever tried network marketing NEEDS THIS BOOK!

To your success,

Dave Vass
Co-authored by Doug Vass
Zfreedom™

978-0-595-49359-3
0-595-49359-9

Printed in the United States
110842LV00003B/51/P